Shades
of Tulsa

An Anthology
by Tulsa NightWriters
www.nightwriters.org

Edited by
Pat Wade and Joan Rhine

To Helen —
a wonderful hostess.
I'm glad I made the
"Great Decision" to join
your group.
                    p. 141

AWOC.COM Publishing
Denton, Texas

Laureen
Tulsa 17 Feb 2008

TABLE OF CONTENTS

PREFACE

One of the best things about a writing community is the sharing—of ideas, of talents, of lives. For more than 50 years, the Tulsa NightWriters have been meeting and sharing these very things, and with this collection, they share with you, their reader.

The stories in this collection reflect the work of our members, highlighting the many paths that the theme *shades of Tulsa* can take along the writer's journey. From the memories of what we've left behind to the places we are going, this anthology showcases our singular city and the stellar writers who live within its bounds, many of whom make a living every day with their prose.

In this centennial year of Oklahoma's statehood, we honor the stories of Tulsa—in fiction, non-fiction, and poetry. We hope you enjoy reading them as much as we have enjoyed sharing them with you.

Pat Wade and Joan Rhine, Editors

Shades

It is a good sign—the first in many moons, the first since leaving the beloved <u>etvlwv vcule</u>, the old nation.

Spirit of the Fire: 1836
by M. Carolyn Steele

A winged shadow floats across patches of sun-dappled ground, appearing and disappearing in the shadows cast by great gnarled oaks. The man stops, unsure of what he has seen, and sucks in his breath as the large shadow appears again, silent, majestic. He leans back, blinking in the glare of morning sun, scanning the sky for a glimpse of what he knows is there.

"Ah ha," he says and smiles. It is a good sign—the first in many moons, the first since leaving the beloved *etvlwv vcule*, the old nation. Behind them, a thousand miles to the east, are their farms and orchards in a place called Alabama. Now the *wvcenvlke*, the white man, lives on the land and picks the fruit, plows the ground, sits at the tables of the pushed-away Creeks. Only the bones of the ancestors remain to claim what had been theirs since before memory.

"What is it, Achee," an old woman at his elbow says and pulls at the hem of his long calico shirt. "Tell me what you see."

"*Lvmhe*, the eagle," he answers for the one whose eyes no longer have sight. He watches until the eagle disappears beyond the lofty treetops.

The ground grumbles beneath his feet. "They are coming," he says to the sightless one before she can ask. "The scouts return."

Others stop beside them and drop their bundled belongings, anxious to rest a moment. Wagons, pulled by long-eared horses, called mules by the white man, creak to a halt. Those sick with the coughing disease, dysentery, pneumonia, complaints too numerous to mention, and those lame with age and frost-injured feet stumble out of the wagons. Mothers and fathers slide young children from their backs.

"Are we there yet? Is this the place the Yuchi and the Wasace told us of? Have we walked far enough?" Questions spill from their mouths, lap over each other, become a chant that rolls back along the hundreds of weary marchers.

"The river, the river!" The horsemen rein their jaded ponies to a halt, and point to the west. Their shout outraces the chant, and people limp, hobble, run for a view of the long walk's end.

The man shifts the deerskin sling containing an earthen pot to his other shoulder. Each day he carries this weight containing the coals and ashes from the last sacred fire kindled in their homeland. And, each night of the forced removal, he starts a new fire from these coals. In this way, the fire's spirit moves with the people, warming them, cheering them, reminding them they are the *Locvlke*, the Turtle Clan.

He climbs to the crest of a small knoll. Maple trees and gray-barked hickories crowd up under tall oaks. Through a tangle of branches and swaging vines, the broad expanse of the Arkansas River sparkles, marking the upper boundary of the Creek Nation, the land set aside for them by the government. Here they will be safe from the encroachment of the white man. It has been promised.

"So, this is it?" asks the old woman, still hanging onto his shirt. She lifts her nose and breathes deeply, testing the air.

"Yes," the man answers and looks up into a large oak with long sturdy arms reaching in all directions. The limbs move, stirring the air, whispering.

The old woman squats and pushes a layer of leaves aside, runs her fingers along the ground. She lifts a pinch of dirt, sniffs it, and touches her tongue to the dirt.

"Humph," she grunts.

"Do you hear the tree talking to us?" he asks the old woman as he helps her stand. "It welcomes us. This is a fair land, pleasant to the eyes. The hills swell and roll, dressed by trees of every description. We will grow our corn and squash here as we did in the land of our ancestors."

"Humph," the old woman grunts again. "I can taste the blandness in the soil, Achee. It does not have the spirit of the people."

"No, not now," he says and leads her to sit with other weary travelers. "But, it will have."

He places his hands on the deep-ridged bark of the tree that talks, feeling its heartbeat, remembering a similar tree, a great tan oak. It stood in their tribal town of Lochapoka in Alabama, a sentinel to the councils and ceremonies of the tribe.

This is a fine tree, he thinks, patting the trunk. He reaches into the earthen vessel, dipping his hand into the still warm contents and scoops out a palm full of ashes. A plume of fine powder rises from the disturbance as he allows the ashes to shift through his fingers, scattering the remnants of the previous night's fire around the oak.

When all that remains in the vessel are chunks of charred wood harboring the fire spirit, he calls for fresh timber to kindle a new fire. Young men hurry as he directs them to dig a pit centered on the crest of the hill, north of the new Council Tree, line it with rocks, and pack a layer of soil on top. He places four logs on the prepared site, each pointing a different direction— north, south, east, west.

"We have come a long way," he says to the men and women who gather. Some sit on their horses or the backs of wagons, others on the ground, a tired people who have forgotten how to smile. "The blood of our feet stains the trail from our homeland. In time the stain will disappear. But the bones of our loved ones, who died along the way, will always remain as lonely markers that we passed. Those of us who survived our long walk will not forget them. We will not forget our traditions."

Sweeping his arm toward the forest of trees, he continued, "Here, we will build a new Lochapoka with a town square like the old Lochapoka. Once more summer will come and we will sit beneath brush arbors and celebrate the Green Corn. Our officials will hold council and our young people will play ball. After the day's toil, drums will sound and our women will don their turtle shells. Our hearts will be happy. We will sing and dance again. The earth, the trees, the animals will hear our music and be pleased."

He empties the still living embers from the vessel onto the logs and kindles the first sacred fire in the new land. Flames nibble at the wood, tasting the bark. Tiny fingers of fire jump along the timber until it catches, roars to life, and tosses glowing sparks into the air.

Tribal elders join the Bringer of Fire, Micco Achee Yahola, and sit as they did in the old town. Their voices echo his, lifting and falling in solemn cadence. One by one, the people take up the song. It is a song of sadness for those lost along the way, a song of celebration for the end of the long walk from home, a song of hope in the land set aside for them—the land called Indian Territory.

Here, they will remain forever. After all, has the white man not promised the land to them for as long as the water flows and the grass grows?

Footnotes:

In 1836, the Council Oak Tree was said to be a tall and stately tree. One hundred and seventy-one years later, this magnificent tree stands at 1730 South Cheyenne Avenue. In the book, "Footsteps Through Tulsa," it is identified as a post oak, approximately 75 feet in height with the high limb span measuring 85 feet. The base of the trunk measures thirteen feet in circumference with bark one and one-half inches thick. A plaque commemorates the long-ago occasion when the people of Lochapoka arrived from the east, scattered their sacred ashes, and made their settlement on a knoll overlooking the bend in the Arkansas River.

In Alabama, Lochapoka was a daughter town to the older settlement of Tvlse. Lochapoka translates to "place of the tortoises" or "the turtling place," a description of the location in the old nation. Since this description no longer fit the new settlement of the transplanted Lochapokans, the village eventually became known as Tulsee Town, a contraction of Tallahassee. Tallahassee was a beloved and ancient tribal town in Alabama. Finally, before the end of the century, Tulsee Town simply became, "Tulsa."

Achee Yahola led the people of Lochapoka tribal town through the tribulations of removal and resettlement. It is said that he built the first cabin for his family near the present intersection of First Street and Frisco Avenue, moving later to a location south and west of the angle formed by the bend in Main Street. He died during the smallpox epidemic of 1850 and rests in an unknown grave in this area.

M. Carolyn Steele retired from a commercial art career to pursue a love of writing. Historical eras, specifically Civil War and Native American, capture her imagination. She has won numerous writing awards and has stories published in various anthologies. Combining her knowledge of storytelling and genealogy, she presents programs designed to inspire others to preserve their family legends.

My foot slipped, and I lost my balance, teetered on the stone's uneven surface, and then plunged, feet first into the river.

River Crossing
by M. M. Coley

Below me, the chocolate water snaked its way through the wide sandy bed of the Arkansas. The river licked at the black stones of the old crossing as if they were bits of licorice.

People said that ancient mammoth bones and spear points sometimes appeared in the rocky river bed near downtown Tulsa. Others told stories of sandbars that pulled things down into the bottomless depths. All kinds of things turned up in that river.

Tomorrow, I would be one of them.

Fresh, moist air blew across the river from the northwest. Frog songs rose, then faded, then rose again as the males and females called to one another from opposite banks. Roaring engines, squealing tires and blaring horns meant the traffic wasn't yet done for the day on Highway 75.

I smoothed my brown hair back with my fingers and wrapped a pink scrunchie around it to form a pony tail, then pulled a denim shirt from the backseat of the car to cover my white camisole. The wind verged on chilly for September. When I looked at the river again, bits of mist hovered over the warm water and seemed to thicken.

What had this grassy hillside looked like two centuries ago, long before Tulsa was settled? Back then Native Americans lived here; traders, trappers and even explorers visited. The America Frontier was expanding, and adventure—and the open, free spaces that it required—was there for the taking.

It had been so different, so unlike today's fast-paced, cluttered, crowded, and impersonal world. Nobody really cared about anyone but themselves. I'd been fired from my newspaper job because of my tendency to want to 'fictionalize,' and my boyfriend of a year had just moved out of my condo and in with someone he'd told me many times was 'just a friend.' The story of my life, repeated ad nauseam.

13

My sandals slipped on the long, wet grass as I stepped down toward the river in the deepening twilight.

The dark stones that formed a natural causeway across this curve of the ancient river jutted up out of the sand. This crossing had been used by everyone from French traders, to Washington Irving during a visit in 1832, and by countless Native Americans and frontiersmen. I imagined I could feel the excitement of that time beneath my feet as I moved to the water's edge.

I stepped out onto the first of the wide crossing stones. Behind me the sounds of the city and the nearby expressway softened. The moon peeked out of a cloud bank to turn the surface of the river shimmering silver. An owl hooted and the river gurgled.

This river, called the Arkansas, would cause a city to be located here, and that city would thrive to become Tulsa. The people who had created this country, this state, and this city had been intent on adventure, looking to find a new life, to leave old ways and old cities behind.

That didn't seem possible for me anymore. The desire even to try was gone. Fate seemed stacked against me.

I stepped onto the next rock and then the next and the next until the river flowed around me on all sides, and there was only the stone path ahead and the stone path back. The swirling mist had swallowed everything else. I stood for a moment.

Odd shadows moved on the far shore. Animals? People? Flickers from a campfire?

I didn't want to go back; I didn't see any need to go forward. I shifted my weight. My foot slipped, and I lost my balance, teetered on the stone's uneven surface, and then plunged, feet first into the river. Thankfully, it was shallow, only ankle deep. But when I tried to step back up on the rock, the sand clutched my feet and took hold. I struggled to lift myself. It was as if something had grabbed onto me and was pulling me down. My legs sank to mid-calf in the slurping sand.

"Help!" I cried. "Quicksand!"

In the still night around me the frogs screamed and some night bird squawked. I lifted my arms to the starry sky. The sand licked at my knees.

If I struggled, the sand would pull me deeper. I forced my body to be still. I called again, "Help!"

"Grab hold," a gruff voice said. A stick poked into my outstretched hand.

I grasped the branch with both hands. The sand tugged at my legs as inch by inch I rose out of the sand. My knees touched the rock. Arms grabbed hold of my shoulders and lifted me up onto my muck-covered sandals.

"Thank you." I squeaked out the words, breathless. My heart pounded, and my head felt light, as if it could disconnect and float away from my body.

"This way. Are ye daft, crossing the stones in the dark?" The man's full beard hung to his chest, a mix of curling brown, red, and silver hairs that glinted in the moonlight. He was only a few inches taller than me.

With long strides, he crossed the stones toward the far shore. In the mist beyond, light flickered and shadows moved.

I followed him to the rocky shore and stepped off the last crossing stone and onto the beach. The mist parted.

"Who's it?" A lurking shadow grew solid into a tall man.

"It's me, McGraw, and some river rat," my companion answered. "Nary to worry on. This 'un looks harmless enough."

"But spies could be afoot. This crossing's known, and not a good place to camp. We need to move, I say." The second man was a good six inches taller than the first man, with long black hair and short, sparse graying stubble.

"In this mist? We'd just as like end up in the sand as this whelp here."

The two men glared at one another. The bearded man motioned with his hand. "Come on. Dry yer breeches by the fire." He looked back at me in the flickering light from the camp fire. "And what kind of breeches be those?" His look moved from my sandals to my capris, then up to my smooth face. His eyes narrowed.

In the firelight, I could now see that the two men wore white shirts with wide mutton-leg sleeves. Their pants and knee boots were smeared with mud. Some of the river's resident homeless?

I glanced quickly around at the rest of the camp. A third man stood up by the fire. His clothes looked as if they had been out of fashion for at least a hundred years, if not two hundred, and they badly needed washing.

"Good eve to ye," he said. His eyes moved curiously over me, and I pulled the open denim shirt closed over my camisole top and buttoned it.

He motioned me toward the fire and waited for me to sit before he eased down onto the huge log. He pulled a pouch from inside one jacket pocket and a pipe from the opposite one. I watched as he filled the pipe and compressed the tobacco. He held a blazing twig like a match to his pipe. As he sucked on the pipe stem the tobacco caught fire, and smoke swirled up around his head.

"A spy, I say!" A voice growled behind me.

"Dressed like 'at! T'is a wench!" McGraw insisted.

"Then I'll warm my bed with her tonight!"

"I saw her first, Houston! Saved her from the sand, I did!"

"Enough!" The third man yelled from his seat by the fire. He exhaled a plume of pipe smoke and looked over at me.

"So what are ye, a wench or a spy?"

"Neither." I sat, back straight, knees together, arms folded, and kept my eyes on the fire. This didn't look good. Three homeless men, and it appeared only one of them could be reasoned with. I looked back over my shoulder to where I knew the river to be but saw only the wisps of fog swirling into the dark night. Why couldn't I see the headlights and hear the traffic on the bridge and expressway?

"Neither? What are ye, then?" The man pulled his pipe out of his mouth and leaned my way. Deep lines etched his face, and gray strands streaked his shoulder-length brown hair. Curious dark eyes peered at me.

"I was out for a walk. I live on the other side of the river."

The other two men shuffled closer to the fire.

"You live on the other side of the river? Alone?" McGraw asked.

They didn't need to know that as of today, I did live alone. "In Tulsa," I answered.

"Tulsa? Where would that be?" the pipe smoker asked.

"There—on the other side of the Arkansas River."

The man looked at me with even more curiosity. Then he peered into the dark night toward where Tulsa should have been.

A howl sliced through the surrounding mist. The two other men huddled closer near the fire.

"Catamount!" Houston whispered hoarsely.

"Aye, or could be the Headless One." The firelight caught the whites of McGraw's eyes. "The one what ye told us about." He nodded at the pipe-smoking gentleman.

The man on the end of my log coughed, and then smiled as he looked into the fire.

Odd how I'd just been thinking about Washington Irving minutes before, and it was he who had written the classic story about Sleepy Hollow two centuries earlier, before his own adventure through what would become Oklahoma. "You mean the Headless Horseman? The one who chased Ichabod Crane at Sleepy Hollow?"

All three pairs of eyes focused on me.

"You know the tale?" The pipe smoker asked.

"Doesn't everybody? Ghost of the Hussein soldier," I said.

"So ye say." The pipe smoker took a long draw from his pipe, his look still glued to my face.

"Washington Irving," I said, in case they'd forgotten the author's name.

The man on the log sat up straight. He nodded at me. "At your service."

The eerie howl came again. Both men gasped, and the one called Houston lifted his gun and pointed it toward the darkness. "It's coming."

"Most likely it's a bobcat," I said. "I live right by the river, and I've never heard of a headless ghost down here. And no black horses either. But I've heard bobcats."

The man lowered his gun.

I looked at the stranger. He wore knee-high black leather boots with buckles, and a black vest over his white shirt. His black waistcoat was unbuttoned.

I wasn't sure what I'd stumbled into when I'd crossed the rocks to this camp, but there was no way it could be Washington Irving and his travel companions. I couldn't have passed back through two hundred years as I stepped across the old river crossing. Could I?

"You're familiar with my work, then?" The gentleman asked.

I stared. "You're Washington Irving, the writer?" The guy *looked* like he could be Washington Irving.

"The same. I'm touring the prairies. It's my next book."

"Well, ain't this something, she's 'eard of him," Houston snickered.

"And I'm not surprised that you haven't," I retorted. Why would Irving be traveling with these two? I wondered if his party had gotten split up and somehow he'd ended up with them temporarily. That is, if I had indeed stepped back two hundred years.

The man who called himself Washington Irving smiled.

"Sassy," my bearded rescuer, McGraw, said.

"Wench," Houston muttered.

"Enough," Irving retorted. "The rest of our party should arrive by morning. I offer you my protection during your stay at our camp. McGraw, Houston, find her some blankets, and get her a biscuit and some stew. This lady is well-read and although her dress and her manner of speech are strange, we shall welcome her. Morning Star, one of our guides, will be glad for another woman's company if you're still here when she returns."

Dawn had tinged the swirling mists purple when I awoke. Irving's blanket was rolled and tied with a leather thong, and he was nowhere in sight. McGraw and Houston were still asleep. Light snores rumbled in their throats.

I got up and crossed the campsite toward the light of dawn. East, I knew, was the direction where the river and Tulsa should be.

Irving was at the water's edge. I stepped up beside him.

"Over there, you say? Tulsa?" he asked.

"Yes." In the dim pre-dawn light, I saw no downtown skyline and no bridges, and heard no cars. "It was there yesterday."

"It's there. You speak of it, so it is. Like the Headless Horseman. You knew of my story. I don't know how, but you knew. That makes the tale real, and my purpose in life is affirmed. And because you speak of Tulsa in your odd speech and clothing, I know that it is also real."

Irving studied the river, and the sky, and the surrounding trees before he spoke again. "There's much I don't understand in this world. And sometimes I feel out of place, in the wrong time. Other times, like here, I'm certain I am in the exact place where God wants me to be. I'll write about this place. People will come here, and your Tulsa will exist."

He turned back toward the camp.

The water shimmered with the dawn, and I could clearly see the black stones, leading across the sand and the water to the opposite shore. I stepped out onto the first and then the second and the third.

I thought about what Irving had said. The Horseman—a story written so long ago—was real because people knew of it. And Tulsa—my city, was real to Irving because of me. His feelings of being out of touch and in the wrong time were my own feelings. A sense of calm filled me.

I stepped onto the next rock. My sandal slipped and my foot slid off the rock and down into the wet sand. I put my hands down to steady myself, pulled my foot back up onto the rock, and hurried on across the stones to the other side of the river.

A car horn beeped up above me, and when I looked up, the bridge spanned the river, and traffic flowed—commuters on their way to work.

I reached the far side and climbed up the bank. As I stepped up to my parked car, I turned back to look at the river crossing; the stones that led to the rocky beach on the other side and a shoreline covered with vegetation and trees. Somewhere, there was a campsite, where Irving and Houston and McGraw had slept.

It would be a good story for me to write.

Mary Coley wrote her first story, *Scruffy the Squirrel*, in the second grade. She's been finding ways to write professionally ever since and has published curriculum and short stories. A Communications Officer with the city of Tulsa, Mary also teaches Environmental Studies for St. Gregory's University College for Working Adults in Tulsa.

She lives on a wooded acre in southwest Tulsa with her husband, Daryl, and three dogs, Gunner, Annie, and Oscar, who appeared at the door and wanted to join the family. She and her husband also have five adult children.

Pepper peered around the corner and up the staircase. Odd, I know what I heard...

The Uninvited Guest
by Jheri Fleet

Pepper spread the photos of her new house on the window seat, fingering them apart. Each print had that same flaw—not in the same place and not the same size. There was nothing to account for the problem. Puzzled, she focused on the new digital camera beside her—*way too expensive to have a problem already.*

Glancing at her watch and then at the snow out front, she realized there was enough time to get to Utica Square and exchange it before closing time.

A sound of heavy footsteps drew her attention. It sounded like someone going upstairs, but she was alone. This had happened several times since she moved in two weeks ago. Each time she checked, there was nothing. She listened. The footsteps continued.

She picked up her camera and photos, rose, and crossed the thickly padded carpet to the living room doorway.

The footsteps stopped.

Pepper peered around the corner and up the staircase. *Odd, I know what I heard...* She walked into the hall and looked upstairs. Even the lighted Christmas tree on the entry table, her only homage to the season, didn't illuminate the top of the stairs.

Pepper listened.

Nothing.

She flipped on the upstairs light switch.

Nothing.

With an exasperated sigh, she inhaled the scent of Black Cavendish pipe tobacco—a pleasant aroma. *There's that odor again...here in the entry this time.* Flipping off the upstairs lights, she walked around the staircase, and through the back hall, taking her coat from the hook by the backdoor. *I have to get used to these annoying, new-to-the-house sounds and odors.*

In minutes, she was at Utica Square. Thirty minutes later, she opened the back door, laid her purse and keys aside, hung

21

her coat, then opened the replacement camera box, loaded the batteries and the new disk.

The phone rang.

"Hi, it's Kali," the cheerful voice said. "Want to grab a bite, or have you eaten?"

"Not yet. I'm taking interior shots of the house to e-mail everyone at the firm."

"Thought you did that a couple of days ago…."

"I did. But every one of them had a white circle or thingy in it somewhere, one has this patch of fog in the middle of my bed, really odd—and there was a white fog funnel coming out of a vent in my study. I got another camera, and I'm going to re-shoot everything.

"Hmm. Still have the photos?"

"Uh-huh."

"I'd like to show them to a friend of mine."

"A camera whiz?"

"Not exactly," Kali said.

"Maybe your friend can tell me what I did wrong."

"I'll bring takeout and be there in a few."

Before Pepper could say goodbye, Kali hung up.

As she moved from room to room taking photos, thoughts of some of the strange occurrences teased her nerves, *footfalls on the stairs, the mantle clock that struck correctly at all times except, for no apparent reason, at 2:34 in the afternoon, the occasional pipe smell, and the scratchy sound of an aria from Tosca on an old Victrola that her brother attributed to the air-conditioning.*

She paused in the dining room studying the harlequin marble floor and fountain in the alcove.

Musing about all the fine parties with important guests that must have occurred here in the last ninety-five years, Pepper wondered about the former owner, the wealthy oil man, known for his lively colleagues, opinions and politics. *Wonder what he was really like*, she thought, remembering some of her research about the house.

She raised her camera and took a shot from the doorway, forgetting too late the oversized-mirror facing the door. *Oh well, I'll have a picture of myself in my new home.*

The photos of the fireplace and library were impressive, as were the shots through open windows of the well-manicured gardens. It was mid-afternoon and already starting to get dark. A half-hour later she finished and went to the study, put the camera disk in the card reader and moved the mouse, bringing the computer screen to life.

By the time Kali arrived, Pepper had printed and checked the new shots. Something was still wrong.

"Hope you've got Thai." Pepper said opening the front door.

"No. Mejicano. This is Tanner," Kali said, waving over her shoulder.

Tanner smiled; Pepper nodded.

"Mexican's fine. I'm starving." Pepper led the way to the kitchen where the photos were arranged on the counter.

"So how are the new photos?" Kali asked.

"Strangest thing…most have the same white bubbles and jiggle things."

"Jiggle things? Is that a technical photographic term?" Kali teased.

Pepper shrugged.

Her friend studied the photos in the first group and then the second, passing them to Tanner who seemed to show great interest in certain ones.

"What do you think it is? It can't be light entering the camera—the camera's digital. One is taken in an almost dark room, and another misfired completely."

"What's this?" Kali held up a solid black photo, and one of the bedroom in what looked like all red lights.

"Go figure. I didn't do anything different for either of those."

"Can you remember what you were thinking… or feeling when you took these?" Tanner asked.

"Sure. I was thinking when Dad's house sells I'll have enough money to tear out all that paneling in the bedroom and paint it lighter more feminine colors, and … make other changes. The dark wood makes me feel like I'm sleeping in a law library."

Pepper shook her head as a frown furrowed her brow. "Strangest thing. It was about that time … that I … smelled the pipe smoke." She snickered. "I had this breath spray in my pocket," she said, producing the cylinder. "I gave the air around me a shot. The next photo came out all red. Must have gotten some in the camera lens."

Kali and Tanner exchanged glances.

"What is it?" Pepper asked.

"You tell her, Tanner," Kali said, shoving the sleeves of her sweater up her arm.

There was a long silence.

"Well?" Pepper leaned forward.

"You probably have an uninvited guest…who isn't ready to leave," Tanner said.

Pepper looked from one to the other, "You're kidding, right?" She could tell they weren't.

"Think of him as a…ghost of Christmas…past." Kali smiled.

"I don't believe in ghosts!" Pepper said.

"Seriously," Tanner turned to Pepper. "I've been ghost hunting for years and have had some real success getting rid of them.

Pepper pulled some paper plates out of the cabinet, opened the sack, and distributed the food. Handing everyone a plate, she led them to the solarium where they sat on the heated flagstone steps as Tanner explained ghosts.

Laying a photo on the step, he pointed to the little foggy, white tornado coming out of a vent, "That's called a vortex. Can you see the circles within circles in it? That's fast movement, and you caught it all in less than a second. Think about that."

"Why would the air be so tremulous in that one place?" Pepper asked.

"It's not air movement, Pepper. That is an uninvited guest moving about. Since it is the master bedroom, I'd bet it's a former owner." He paused, "Anyone die in this house?"

"The first owner did," Pepper said.

Tanner pulled another photo to his side. "This," he pointed to the large round clear circle in the master bedroom, looking much like a huge soap bubble. "This is an orb. The easiest ghosts to see look like this. Any flash camera can get one of these."

"In the game room there were four," Pepper said.

"That makes sense," Tanner said, shifting through other photos. "People come, have fun, and never want to leave, or old friends come …even after they cross over." He took a bite of chalupa and chewed as he thought. He swallowed and looked at Pepper, "What do you know about the house?"

"Quite a bit. I've been interested in it since I was in law school. It was built and owned by Morgan Monahans until his death. Since then it sat empty for ten years while his heirs fought over it, and then there were six owners in quick succession. I've been trying to buy it for a year while it sat empty. Finally got it for my price."

Tanner and Kali exchanged knowing smiles.

Kali laughed. "Like you, the others moved in before they met the ghost of 'Christmas past'. They couldn't tell anyone or they wouldn't be able to unload the house. Oh maybe close friends, but not the realtor."

"What can I do?" Pepper asked.

"There are a lot of things to do. First you need to smudge the house."

Pepper's face contorted, "Smudge?"

"A Native American ceremony to clear the space of unwanted energy," Kali said.

"And that does it? No more white spots on photos or ghosts of Christmas past?"

"Should work..." Tanner nodded.

"How will I know if it worked?"

Tanner held up the photo Pepper took in the harlequin marble dining room. "Who helped you take the photos?"

"No one."

Tanner turned the photo to face Pepper, "So, who's the guy in the mirror."

Without looking, Pepper said, "Me."

"No. I mean the one behind you."

"Don't be ridiculous. I was alone…."

Pepper looked, gasped and reached for the photo. She saw the face in the mirror behind hers. Not transparent or a foggy unclear shape, but as clear…as alive as she was…a man a foot taller, with broad strong shoulders and a square face framed by thick graying hair and as clear and human as she was in the photo. "He's alive...and he's…still handsome…." Her voice tailed off.

"Think that's Monahans?" Tanner asked.

Without taking her eyes off the man in the photo, Pepper shrugged.

Kali watched her friend carefully study the photo.

Tanner flipped through other photos. "Here he is again on the big brass door hinge. They can be seen on shiny surfaces too. Go back and look at family gatherings, they love those. They come in as fog, odd neon-like light forms, and orbs."

"No way..." Pepper exhaled as though the wind had been knocked out of her. In the photo of the door hinge, the man's arms were folded across his chest and, he was turned to the side looking down at her, smiling.

"Want to smudge the house this evening? It's an optimum time to do it." Tanner said. "Full moon tonight."

He waited for a response from Pepper who was staring at the photos in her hand. "Monahans died...twenty years ago...today..." she said barely above a whisper.

"Even better—death anniversary—excellent time. I'll get my stuff out of the car," Tanner said, retracing his steps to the kitchen.

Kali moved closer to Pepper. "Are you all right?"

Pepper nodded mechanically. "I...don't believe in ghosts...but...he's in the picture with me. I took the picture—printed it—no one messed with it. This I know...."

"Don't worry. Tanner will get rid of him, and then you can have this house all to yourself." She resettled, drawing her legs up under chin, put her arm around her friend, and pulled her close. "After all these years living out of bags and catching planes, eating in strange restaurants, and trying cases all over the world...you finally have a home. No small feat for you. How come this is the only house you ever wanted?"

Pepper didn't respond.

"Now you'll be able to settle down and have a life, meet a man and...."

Pepper turned toward Kali, "This," she said shaking the photo at Kali, "is the man I have been looking for. And now...."

Kali stared at her friend, puzzled, "What are you saying, Pepper? Is this the man you were always talking about?"

"Yes!" Pepper nodded emphatically, "When I was in Harvard Law, I came home to visit Mom. She wanted to go to an opening at Philbrook," Pepper said. "I didn't really want to go...but I did." Pepper relaxed against Kali, "I saw him there," her voice became dreamy, "he was standing to one side watching everyone...and then our eyes met...and...we walked through the exhibit together...and talked for over an hour...I fell in love with him. When it was time to go, I went to find Mom, to introduce her to 'her future son-in-law'. But he was just...gone. I never saw him again...until...."

Kali stared at her friend.

"He told me where he lived—here. The next time I came home I drove by, but there was a Sold sign out front. I thought he'd moved away."

Kali pulled away and looked at Pepper. "Hold on!"

"What?" Pepper asked, "What?"

"You were twenty-one then—and you're thirty-six now."

Pepper nodded.

"Then it can't be him, Pepper. First of all Monahans had to be an OLD man when he died, right?"

"So?"

"Twenty years ago he died—an OLD man. You were ONLY fifteen years old—twenty years ago...So he was dead by the time you were twenty-one. Ergo, you never met this Monahans, and he wouldn't have looked this young if you had."

"I did. I'm telling you!" Pepper said, rising abruptly, taking her paper plate and moving quickly through the dark hall to the kitchen. She flipped on the lights. The room seemed freezing cold, but no doors or windows were open.

How can this be? I finally find him again and he's a... a... there has to be some other explanation! She opened the trash and slung the plate inside.

The backdoor opened letting in a gust of chilling wind.

"I'll be ready in a few minutes." Tanner said, "Can I just set these things down in here?"

"Sure..."

The lights in the kitchen went out.

"It's okay, "Tanner said, "I have a flashlight." He turned it on, handed the oversized flashlight to Pepper, struck a match and started to light the smudge stick.

"Before you start." Pepper said, her voice emotional. "Explain exactly what this is going to do."

Tanner shook the match out. "I will get rid of orbs or vortexes in your photos and any previous owners lollygagging around. Trust me, it will be more peaceful here." He struck another match.

Kali rounded the corner. "What happened to the lights?"

Pepper ignored her question and blew out the match. "What...if I don't want him gone, now that I know who it is?"

"Don't be ridiculous," Kali said. "You don't want a ghost living here."

Tanner shrugged. "It's her house."

There was a long silence. Perhaps several minutes passed with no one speaking.

"I'm sorry I wasted your time," Pepper said to Tanner. "But, I want the house... exactly as it is."

The lights flickered on, and the chill disappeared.

Jheri Fleet lives at Pecan Hill in Midland, Texas where she runs a pecan orchard. If there is enough daylight left at the end of the day she creates one-of-a kind silver jewelry designs for her growing clientele and writes in the shade of her trees, on her back terrace, and inside when it is cold. As a freelance journalist she wrote more than one thousand bylined articles, and later, as a public relations counselor, wrote almost as many with client bylines. Her internationally syndicated Knight-Ridder column ran for more than four years under the G. F. Chastain byline.

She was crying quietly, so quietly I couldn't hear her, but I could see the tears on her face, reflecting the bright light of the full moon.

Becky
by Dale Whisman

I was about halfway through my rounds, having patrolled two sides of the enclosed campground. The written job description I had been given when my employer, Tulsa Security, assigned me to the post simply stated I was to patrol the ten foot chain-link fence at least once each hour between sundown and sunrise. At this time of year that meant about nine trips around the perimeter of the ten-acre campground, site of the Winnifred P. Austin Summer Camp for Young Girls.

Winnifred Austin had been a wealthy business woman, and her ancestors were among the original founders of old Tulsy Town, later renamed Tulsa, one of Oklahoma's finest cities. Having no children of her own, Winnifred donated much of her holdings to various civic projects, especially those directed at youth. The ten-acre camp had once been the site of the original Austin homestead and was located just outside the city limits, bordering a large wooded area.

I was on my third round of the night. Perspiration soaked through my blue uniform shirt. August in Oklahoma meant heat and humidity, even at night. The girls called me Old Man Mullins, and I guess I was starting to feel the years, especially during the summer months. I was looking forward to getting back to the lodge and a well-stocked ice chest.

It was eleven-fifteen when I saw her. She was about nine years old, a little younger than most of the girls at the summer camp. She was dressed in a pale blue nightgown, with tiny white bows at the collar, and her blonde hair was braided in pigtails reaching to her shoulders.

She was crying quietly, so quietly I couldn't hear her, but I could see the tears on her face, reflecting the bright light of the full moon. She had every right to be crying. Here she was, out in the woods some two hundred yards from the house, barefoot, and long past her bedtime.

29

"There now, sweetheart, what are you doing out here all alone? Are you sleepwalking? Trying to run away? Come here, darlin', I'll take you back to the house. You should be in bed, sound asleep, dreaming of dolls and swings, and chocolates. Don't be afraid. My name's Mike, what's yours?"

"Rebecca." Her voice was so soft I read her lips more than heard her speaking. She almost smiled at me. Then she shook her head, turned away, and stepped behind a bush, disappearing into the darkness.

"Here! Come back, Rebecca. You can't go running around out here like this."

Pulling the five-cell flashlight from my belt I hurried forward flashing the light around the small clearing; the girl was nowhere in sight.

I searched, Lord, how I searched! I called, the flashlight probing into every shadow, checking behind every tree and shrub, but the girl was nowhere to be found. Finally, I knew I had to advise Ms. Norris what had happened, though I certainly wasn't looking forward to that!

Using the handheld citizen's band radio I called the main house and roused Ms. Norris after a brief pause.

"This is Mike, with Security. I'm sorry to bother you at this hour, but it seems one of the girls has wandered out of the house, and is lost in the woods. I saw her, just for a moment, then she was gone. I've looked everywhere, but I can't find her. I thought you might want to..."

"All right, Mike. I'll wake the others, and we'll come out to help look. Where are you, exactly?"

In less than ten minutes, four of the camp councilors and Ms. Norris herself had joined me in searching the campground. But after a full hour, having covered every square foot of the enclosure, we had to admit the girl was simply not there.

"Who was she, Mike? Did you recognize her? Did she speak to you at all?"

"Well, Ms. Norris, I asked her name, trying to make friends with her, you know? And I think she said her name was Rebecca. Or it could have been Roberta. I couldn't really hear her very well, I never got that close. She seemed to be afraid of something. I tried not to scare her, I really did."

"I'm sure you did, Mike. Stop worrying, it's not your fault. We've just got to find her."

"Well, ma'am, she's not out here. And she didn't go through the gate, because I locked both gates at sundown, just like always. And she didn't go through or under the fence. I know every foot of that fence, and it's in good shape. Believe me, she's still got to be in camp, somewhere."

Bobbie, one of the councilors, suggested, "Maybe she went to the lodge and crawled back into bed." They decided there was no choice. They had to find her even if it meant waking the rest of the girls.

At the lodge, Ms. Norris sent the councilors around for a bed check. They reported all the beds were in use and everyone appeared to be accounted for. But of course, that wasn't good enough. It was decided everyone would be awakened, and assembled in the cafeteria, for a head count.

The sleepy campers showed a mixture of emotions at being dragged out of bed at one in the morning. If the truth were known, a few of them hadn't yet been asleep, as young girls have a tendency to lie awake and giggle at summer camp. Some were grouchy, some a little afraid and had to be consoled by their councilors. A few seemed thrilled by the adventure.

"Girls! Everyone sit down and remain where you are. And be quiet! Nancy, would you count heads? Marie, please go to my office and get the roster. Thank you."

By the time the count was finished and the roster retrieved, a few little heads were resting on table tops, and others were close together engaged in wild speculation as to what was going on.

"I count thirty-seven, Ms. Norris."

"Thank you. Well... now just a minute. I have only thirty-six on the list. Count them again Nancy. Marie, you count them too. Girls! Stop moving around. The sooner you settle down the sooner we'll be through, and you can get back to bed."

"I'm sorry, Ms Norris, but I still count thirty-seven."

"Me too."

An exasperated pause followed. From a corner of the room, I made my own count. Thirty-seven.

Ms. Norris pulled me aside. "Mike, do you see the girl in the room?"

"No, ma'am. I've been looking close, but I don't think she's here. If she is, she's not wearing the same gown."

Ms Norris took time to count the names on the roster. Thirty-six. She counted them again, and got the same answer.

"Well, we can settle this soon enough. Girls, I am going to call your names. When I do you are to stand up and cross the room to the tables over there, and sit quietly until I have finished. All right... Martha Anderson... Linda Arnold... Barbara Benson... "

One by one the number of girls on one side of the room grew fewer, while the group on the other side grew larger... and quieter. The girls were beginning to understand that something serious was going on.

"Cathy Webster... Denise Williams... Darlene Williams... and Julia Young. That's everyone, right?"

"Thirty six names, Ms Norris. I counted."

"Yes, thank you, Nancy. Marie, did you..."

Marie stood near the now very quiet group of girls at the far side of the room. She was pale, and her voice broke as she said, softly... "Thirty-seven. I count thirty-seven. We have one girl too many!"

A few of the girls started to cry, a few others joined in, and they all started to look around at one another and draw apart.

"Excuse me, Ms. Norris, could I ask a question?" It was Ida Claymore, the camp cook.

"Of course, Ida. What is it?"

"Mike, where were you when you saw her?"

"I was about halfway around, over in the northeast corner, just past... Oh! Oh... well now..."

"What is it?" Ms. Norris asked.

"That's right above Becky's Bluff, ma'am." Ida spoke softly, as though embarrassed to mention it at all.

"Becky's... Why, that's absurd. You don't think...?" Ms. Norris hesitated, then turned to the councilors. "Marie, you and Nancy get the girls calmed down. Play a game or something."

"Yes'm" Marie replied, her eyes wide as she watched Ms. Norris, Ida, and me hurry from the cafeteria enroute to the front office.

"Becky's Bluff?" I asked. "That's where the little Williams girl was found. But that was... that was almost fifteen years ago."

Ms. Norris was behind her desk, fingers nervously tapping the arm of her swivel chair as Ida and I stood by, waiting.

"I won't have it. This is neither the time, nor the place for this sort of irresponsible speculation. There are no such things as ghosts, and you both know it!"

"Yes ma'am" we answered in unison, but without conviction.

"That little girl fell off the cliff years ago, long before this camp was ever built, and from what I've heard, it was just an accident—a tragic accident to be sure, but an accident nonetheless. She would have absolutely no reason to hang around here and... What the hell am I saying? There's no such thing as ghosts!"

"I was there, you know." Ida almost whispered.

"What? You were there? What do you mean?"

"I was there when it happened. I worked for them. I was their housekeeper. I helped... I helped raise Becky. She was such a sweet little..." Tears filled Ida's warm eyes, and her voice broke.

"What really happened, Ms. Claymore?" I asked.

"We were never sure, but they thought little Becky got out of bed in the middle of the night and went out to find her puppy, Tag. It was a warm summer night, just like...like tonight. And she loved that pup so... she wandered over to the bluff, and... and fell. They found her broken body at the base of the cliff. Tag, the puppy was with her. Mr. Williams heard the pup barking and whining." Ida began crying again as she added "They brought her home and laid her in her own little bed, just as I had done the night before. She was so lovely in her pigtails, and her little blue gown, with...."

"With tiny white bows at the collar..." I added, remembering what I was beginning to think of as a vision.

The two women stared at me as the intercom buzzed.

"Yes?" Ms. Norris spoke into the intercom.

Nancy's voice sounded a little shaky coming through the speaker, "Ms. Norris, we just counted again, and now we get thirty-six. We counted three times, and we get thirty-six."

There was a pause, as the three of us looked questioningly at one another. "Put them back to bed," Ms. Norris said. "It's all a mistake. Just a mistake." But none of us really believed that.

Ms. Norris and the councilors eventually got the girls resettled in bed, and the lodge grew quiet. I went back out to patrol the fence—and look for Becky.

Well, sir, that was twelve years ago. I decided I was too old for security work, pretty much too old for anything, so I retired right after that, and bought this cabin. It's not much, but it's home for me and Tag. That's right, I got me a dog, and named him Tag, like Becky's pup. I thought...well, it doesn't make sense when you say it out loud, but I thought if there was a dog around, a dog named Tag, Becky would, just maybe, you know, would maybe not be so... so lonely, I guess.

And it seems to work. We're just about a quarter mile from Becky's Bluff, and Tag and me go over there a couple of times a week. There's a creek there where I fish sometimes, but mostly we just sit under a tree and wait. And sure enough, every once in a while Becky comes by. She still doesn't talk to me, but at least she doesn't cry any more. And she seems awfully happy to see Tag.

Tulsa native Dale Whisman is an experienced stage and screen actor as well as an award-winning novelist, playwright, and screenwriter. His feature length film, *Down The Road*, won Best Feature Filmed on Oklahoma Soil at the BareBones Script-2-Screen Film Festival in Tulsa in 2005, and his screenplay *Hookers* won the award for Best Short Screenplay at the BareBones Script-2-Screen Film Festival in Tulsa in 2006.

... I saw no one and heard only the distant sound of the engine, laboring in the belly of the ship.

Star of Texas
by Bob Avey

"No refunds," the man said. He shoved a receipt across the counter, then handed me a room key.

I stood in some sort of lobby, a hole in my memory holding the details of how I'd come to be there. I looked around, paying particular attention to the casino posters, then slid my hand around the prescription bottle in my pocket, making a mental note to speak with Doctor Green when I got back to Tulsa.

The man grinned. "It ain't like they're going to sail this rust bucket to the Bahamas or anything. Just far enough, to make the gambling legal then return to port. You'll be back on solid ground by eight o'clock tomorrow morning."

I walked down the ramp and crossed the gangplank, and when I stepped onboard, I remembered leaving Tulsa—South Texas my destination.

The ship rose and fell slightly. Then, while glimmers of light dotted the sky and a partial moon hung over the horizon, the Star of Texas pulled gracefully out of Galveston Bay. I was in for a long night, and to make matters worse, I had attracted the interest of a man who watched me like a pickpocket might study his mark. Seconds later, he pushed away from the railing and approached.

"First time out?" he asked. A coating of grease held his hair in place.

"Yeah," I said. I tried to act as if it didn't bother me, but the expression on his face said he wasn't buying it.

He grinned around the edges of his cigarette, then pulled a tin box from his pocket and popped it open. Inside were some mints and a few small, white pills. "Want one?"

I shook my head.

With his finger, he shoved one of the pills around the bottom of the tin. "You can't get no sicker than what the sea gives you. You take one of these, you won't even know you're on the water."

35

I changed the subject. "So, this casino I heard about. Where do I find it?"

"Don't matter at the moment. They don't open the doors until we reach federal waters."

He disappeared into the crowd, and I went to an outside cantina where I grabbed a napkin from the bar and wiped perspiration from my forehead.

Flashing a grin, the bartender popped open a beer, then set it on the counter. "Perhaps this will cool you off, man." He spoke with a Jamaican accent.

I stuffed a dollar in the tip jar, but the beer slid down my throat as if it were laced with warm motor oil, and I'd only taken one swallow when someone touched my shoulder.

"Allen?"

I turned toward the sound of my name, and everything fell into place.

"Allen Carver. It is you. I hoped you would come." She wore gold earrings shaped like roses.

My pulse quickened, but the distant look in her eyes sent a feeling of sadness through me. Heavy makeup covered a bruise on her cheek. "It's good to see you again," I said.

I embraced her in a hug that sent an all too familiar pain through my heart. I remembered a time fifteen years ago, standing in her backyard, just out of reach of the porch light.

Hearing footsteps, I turned to see the slick-haired man who'd tried to sell me drugs.

"What the hell's going on here?"

Laura glanced at the man, released her hold, and stepped away. "This is my husband, Rico."

I felt my face redden. Just like old times. "Laura and I are old friends," I said, "went to the same school in Tulsa."

My choice of words earned me a glare from Laura. I'd intentionally left out the word *together*.

"Small world," he said. He grabbed Laura's arm. "You coming with me?"

I watched them walk away and felt a wave of nausea. *Must be the smell of seawater and diesel fuel.* I turned to the bartender, "Say, buddy. How do I find the casino?"

He pointed to a door behind the cantina. "Through there, man."

The doorway led to the interior of the ship. A long corridor lined with numbered doorways unfolded in front of me, and as I walked along the wine-colored carpets, I was reminded of an old residence hotel. I half expected to see tenants leaning against the dark paneled walls, and to hear voices coming from within the rooms, but I saw no one, and heard only the distant sound of the engine, laboring in the belly of the ship.

Near the end of the hallway, I descended a set of stairs and entered the casino. I hurried past Rico, who was hunkered over the craps table, then I exchanged money for some tokens at the cashier's cage and sat down at a slot machine.

Some time later I fished another token out of my shirt pocket, and something cold touched my skin. I pulled up a gold chain from which dangled a pendant shaped like a rose. It was wet and smelled of the sea.

"Bet you got that for your sweetheart," the lady next to me said. "Sure is pretty. Bet she is, too."

I handed her my tokens. "More like a missed opportunity."

Rico was still shooting dice. I closed my hand around the necklace and went to look for Laura.

I found her standing by the starboard railing, staring out to sea. Except for the two of us, the deck was empty. Even the enterprising Jamaican had packed it in.

Laura turned and smiled. The glow of the moon cast a reflection that danced in the black eddies of the water and played in the depths of her eyes. "Why are you standing so far away?"

I took a step forward. "Water terrifies me, especially this much of it."

She exhaled softly, as if she wanted to laugh but couldn't quite come to it. "And yet, here you are."

I took another step. My legs shook visibly.

"That's better," she said. "Now all you have to do is look at me."

"I am looking at you."

"You're looking at my shoulders."

I forced myself to look up, feeling the heat of my blush when we made eye contact.

"You're a handsome man, Allen. It's confidence you lack—nothing else."

I showed her the necklace.

Instinctively, her hand went to her throat, and she looked down. "How did you get that?"

"When we met at the bar, it must have slipped from your neck and fallen into my shirt pocket."

"How did you know it was mine?"

"It matches your earrings."

"How nice of you to notice." Her slight smile transformed her, made her even lovelier.

When I dropped the necklace into her hand, fresh marks along her forearm caught my attention.

She jerked away.

"Rico?" I asked.

"Don't worry about Rico. He's in the casino where he'll stay until he's lost all his money. By that time, he'll be so drunk it hardly matters."

"How could you stay with someone like that?"

A look somewhere between anger and resignation flashed across her face. "You don't understand."

"Then why did you send for me, Laura? What do you want?"

She didn't answer, so I continued. "It would've been a nice prom, you know. Do have any idea how it felt, standing there with your father looking down at me like that? I guess I should've known, the way you ignored me at school, turning your head when I walked past, laughing with your friends as if I wasn't there—just some ghost only you could see, brushing down the hallways in search of a life that never was. Why did you put me through that? Filling me with false hope when we were alone, only to dash it when we were at school?"

She brushed my cheek with the back of her hand then shook her head. "I didn't go to the prom with Tony Lathum. Dad made that up. When you came to the door, I was locked in my room all dressed up and ready to go, just like you were. I still have the corsage you gave me."

"Why didn't you tell me?"

She looked away. "I've made a lot of bad choices. But my mother once said if you look at the ocean long enough, you'll find a solution to your problems and bury them at sea."

"What kind of problems are we talking about?"

"In several hours, the ship will return to port, and everyone will gather by the exit. When the gate opens, everyone rushes out. They don't bother to check names."

I thought about that for a moment. "You're not thinking of stowing away?"

"No. I'm sure they check for that. But if you got on and didn't get off, they'd never know."

"I'm not sure I'm following you."

She shook her head. "I'm sorry for the way I treated you. Now go. I need to be alone."

Laura's state of mind troubled me, but I did as she asked. As I crossed the deck, a sickness descended on me. I headed for the door behind the cantina, but it was locked. I edged along the portside deck. The upper decking formed a canopy over the area, and shadows dominated gray-painted equipment, but I suspected it would lead to a side entrance.

Feeling worse, I left the safety of the wall and gripped the outer railing. I leaned forward, the wind whipping my shirtsleeves. My mouth tasted salty. I peered into the black water below, wondering how long it might take for me to hit the water if I lost my balance and fell overboard. Would anyone know about it? No one was around. When I looked out, I saw nothing but an infinite supply of water and darkness.

No one would know.

I could yell, but the sea would swallow me and my cries while the ship sailed on.

Fear overcame sickness. I backed away from the railing and edged along the narrow deck. When I found the entrance, I said a little prayer then stumbled along the hallway until I reached my room.

Once inside, I dug the prescription bottle from my pocket, downed a couple of pills without water, then stripped off my clothes and fell onto the bed.

I'd just dozed off when a sound brought me out awake. I flipped on the light to see Laura standing over me. A thin sheen of perspiration covered her skin, and her dress was torn.

"How did you get in here?"

"That's not important. I found Rico in the casino, drunk and trying to borrow money from a stranger."

She unfastened her dress, letting it slide from her shoulders and fall to the floor. "He could barely walk. I had to help him."

She crawled into bed and switched off the light.

I pulled her close, coveting her presence like a homeless child might cling to the memory of family, and when we made love it was warm, and slow, and beautiful. For the first time in years, hope guided my spirit. At the same time, I expected her to disappear, the warm reality of her substance turning to smoke, which might linger, but only for a moment above my bed.

At some point, I faded off to sleep, and when I awoke, I knew I was alone. I ran my hand across her side of the bed to confirm my fears. A morbid understanding crawled across my senses, and I bolted upright. Laura was gone, but it was her talk of getting on and off the ship without being noticed that bothered me. It wasn't nonsense. Misery showed in her face. Unhappiness laced her words. I struggled into my clothes. She meant to bury her problems at sea all right. She meant to throw herself overboard.

I left my room, hoping I was not too late, but when I stepped outside into the humid air, heavy with the scent of marine life, there were no passengers. I scrambled through the vessel, searching the decks, the hallways, and the lounge areas, but I found no one. I was alone, the only one on board a ship that plunged blindly ahead.

Fear crawled along the base of my spine when I spotted Laura leading her stumbling husband along the portside deck. As I ran toward her, she stepped behind Rico. I called out, begging her to stop, but she didn't seem to hear me. She ran her problem toward the railing and shoved him overboard.

I drew near and reached for Laura, but Rico's hand shot up from behind the railing. He dragged her out of my grasp in a final act of cruelty.

I fell, helpless, against the railing, and watched her disappear into the black water, Rico's grip still firm around her arm.

It was then that someone spoke, and I began to wonder if I had indeed lost my mind. I was no longer on the ship but sat in my car, which was parked alongside the street near the docks.

An old man stared down at me. "You okay, mister?"

"I'm not sure."

I held my cell phone in my hand. I flipped it open. It showed: 8:05 am, 08/25/07. "Where am I?"

"Galveston, Texas. What you been drinking?"

"I don't know."

"Don't surprise me none, not if a man don't know what town he's in. Where you from?"

"Tulsa."

"What you doing down here?"

I pointed toward the water. "I just got off the ship."

"What ship?"

"The Star of Texas."

The old man stared at me "You didn't get off no Star of Texas. That ship ain't sailed out of here for a long time." He turned and walked away.

I leaned back trying to make some sense of things. I saw a piece of paper in my shirt pocket, and I pulled it free. A morbid sickness ran through me as I smoothed it, my eyes scanning the document as if it were an expired lottery ticket with the correct sequence of numbers. I had the receipt the man had given me to board the ship, but the document was wrinkled, yellowed with age, and carried a date of August 25, 1994.

I started the car and turned on the air conditioner. I would never see The Star of Texas again, but when I closed my eyes, I felt the sway of her bow, smelled the exhaust from her engines, and thought of Laura, floating somewhere between time and the vast inky blackness of the Gulf night waters.

Bob Avey is the author of short stories, non-fiction articles, and a mystery titled *Twisted Perception*. He lives with his wife and son in Broken Arrow, Oklahoma where he works as an accountant in the petroleum industry. Visit his web site www.bobavey.com.

Memories

Since they were unregulated, they could run wherever they wished, and so they ran along the railroad lines...

A Nickel Ride in a Jitney
by Dan Case

Ruby and Stella stood shivering next to the newly built tracks of Tulsa's street railway system.

"The streetcar should have been here ten minutes ago," said Stella.

"F-f-fifteen m-m-minutes," stammered Ruby. Her teeth were chattering so hard she could hardly get the words out.

Just then Stella spied the streetcar pull around a corner five blocks away. "I see it now, five more minutes," she said.

"I c-c-can't w-w-ait that long," replied Ruby. She turned to run across the street to a five-and-dime store that was still open, but before she could step off the curb, a black Model-T Ford skidded around the corner, bounced over the railroad track, and stopped in front of Ruby and Stella.

"Hop right in ladies," said the driver. "Ride will cost you a jitney, same as the streetcar—only I'll get you where you're going a lot faster and on time."

Stella and Ruby looked at each other, then into the Model-T. The backseat was full—five people were crammed in there. The driver was in the front along with a high school aged girl and two gentlemen.

"You don't have room," said Stella.

"No problem," said the driver. "You two gentlemen jump out onto the running board and let these ladies get in the front here."

Reluctantly, the men gave up their seats, and Stella and Ruby slid into the automobile. They each dropped a nickel into the driver's hand.

"Hang on out there," yelled the driver. The men on the running board had pulled their hats down on their heads, thrown their coat collars up, and wrapped a gloved hand around whatever they could grab on to.

The jitney jerked forward and swung from the curb, speeding along the railroad tracks. It was two blocks away

44

before the late streetcar pulled to a stop across from the five-and-dime.

An angry conductor stepped out of the empty streetcar long enough to look at his watch and curse the Model-T. No one but the driver was around to hear the curses, but this scene was becoming a daily routine, and he was used to it by now.

These "jitneys" as they were being called were everywhere. They multiplied like a plague to the street railroad companies. Every entrepreneur in Tulsa was putting as many of the private cars onto the streets as he could afford. Unregulated, they could run wherever they wished, and so they ran along the railroad lines where they picked up passengers ahead of the forever-late streetcars.

Since the jitneys could hold seven or more passengers on the inside and three on each running board, the automobiles were a very profitable operation. The problem was that they were taking all the business from the railroads, the Tulsa Street Railway Company, and the Oklahoma Union Railway Company. These companies finally appealed to the city commission for relief, with the result that the city passed a jitney ordinance. The jitneys were licensed and required to post indemnity bonds. Equally important, the ordinance made obligatory the posting of regular routes, which would be removed at least two blocks from the streetcar rail lines. Thus began five years of the regulated jitney era on Tulsa streets.

It didn't take long for the jitney ordinance to be modified. One jitney driver of the day, Ernest Case, said, "The girls would pile up around us drivers so that the city bosses had to pass a law that we was only allowed to haul two in the front seat with us. That way the girls couldn't crowd us to where we couldn't handle the car good. There was a few times folks would fall off the sides, so we was limited to just two on each running board."

With so many owners on each jitney line there was sure to be some conflicts. The organized jitney lines had men who started the jitneys at intervals of a few minutes apart on each line. The drivers, in order to make wages, had to make sure their cars were full most of the time. In order to do this, they would have to race each other down the street, cutting each other off to get the next group of passengers. "We would drag each other and get the other guy's passengers, and when you got out to the end of the line, you could just as well figure on a fight. I carried a black eye most of the time," Ernest said.

The era of the jitneys ended just as fast as it started. The city awarded a bus franchise that covered most of the same streets the jitneys serviced. In only a few weeks, the buses drove the jitneys out of business. It seems people just naturally preferred a comfortable ride in a bus to hanging on the running board of a secondhand car. "I could see the writin' on the wall, and I went down and got me a job working for the bus company," said Ernest Case, one of the last jitney drivers in Tulsa.

Dan Case is the editor/publisher of the award-winning magazine and website for writers, Writing for DOLLARS! Writer's Digest lists Writing for DOLLARS! as one of the "25 Best Places to Get Published Online" and one the "101 Best Web Sites for Writers." Writing for DOLLARS! is published semi-monthly since 1997 and boasts more than 75,000 subscribers. To receive a free subscription, fill out the form online at www.WritingForDollars.com

...just the right look on her face, one of her sly little winks, and I'd again be filled with terror...

The Flying Saucer
by Gloria Teague

Snow day! There can't be many words that fill each heart with abundant joy or lift the spirit of a child more than those two words. Sweet liberty! No teachers, no waiting in the cold for a bus that would be running late, no fears about the homework you hadn't quite finished the previous night.

The next best thing was that all your friends, siblings, and, in my case, cousins just happened to be outside building snowmen and hurling tightly packed snowballs at each other. Some would gather a gang to dare a climb up the highest hills in Tulsa for sledding. Since we had little money, the times I participated, I had to use a cardboard box. It didn't take long for the cardboard to get soggy and fall apart, and it made me the brunt of all their jokes. That was the reason I rarely joined in on those daytime ventures to see who could be first to break a bone. But there was this one night...

It was a glorious, magical, cold but sparkling night. I was sitting in the living room staring into the dark night that pressed at the windows, transfixed by the lace-like patterns of ice crystals growing on the glass panes.

Just a few days after Christmas, this was the night before we had to return to school after the holiday break. I don't know how many kids prayed for a delay in those plans, but God must've been listening for He opened the heavens and let it snow, let it snow, let it snow! By the time it had settled down to flurries, there had to be at least eighteen inches of breathtaking whiteness that assured there would be no school the next day. One last chance to enjoy being free.

On this night we were inside our humble, but cozy, home, and it was late—around eight o'clock. Surely time for all sensible parents to make sure their children were inside safe and warm. But then, my family had always been a little bit different, and I wouldn't have had it any other way.

The top forty was playing on the radio and Mom sang along, belting out "Wellll, since my baby left me, I've found a new place to dwell. It's down at the end of Lonely Street..." when there was a knock on the door. Mom was surprised to see her four nephews standing on the porch, grinning up at her. We knew that along with their parents they'd been visiting Grandma ("You better never call me that! You call me Mamaw.") who lived on the same street. The rest of our family must have been in a charitable frame of mind because, when the younger generation asked to go outside to play, the older generation said, "Sure, knock yourselves out. Please!"

"Aunt Midge, since there's no school tomorrow, can Gloria come out to slide down the hill next to Mamaw's house?"

"Yeah, I guess she can. Wait a minute, and we'll walk back with you. I might as well go visit with the rest of the clan while y'all play."

While Mom pulled our coats and boots out of the closet, I went to find an old cardboard box on the back porch. I stepped out the door and was struck speechless. Silence. It was a hush so deep, so profound that a pine cone dropping from a nearby tree onto the newly-fallen snow seemed an intrusion. The vision of frozen splendor, a whiteness so astounding it appeared blue in the moonlight, took my breath. This was a wonderment that has never diminished for me, and still enthralls me with awe, even though I've become an adult who isn't as easily impressed as I was that snowy night.

I forced myself to go back inside, dragging behind me that ratty green bean box. After cramming a pair of socks onto my hands for gloves, Mom walked in short, tiny steps over the frozen tundra, and the rest of us ran, slid and pushed each other down the street, making our way toward "The Hill." Mom turned left and walked down the steps to her mother's house while we kids walked straight ahead and began to ascend. Mohammed going to the mountain.

Even though the hill was covered with a layer of glimmering packed ice, perfect for sliding, my box was tattered and a sodden ruin within ten minutes. My cousins, who had gotten new sleds for Christmas, began to laugh and tease me. I was mortified and angry that we were too poor to buy a spiffy new sled. And, of course, my cousins wouldn't share any of theirs with a mere girl.

The last trip I made down the hill on that box, I scraped my backside because the cardboard stopped halfway down the hill and my butt kept going.

At the bottom I stood watching the others and thinking how I could find something better to use than a square of cardboard. I conceived what seemed to be a brilliant plan. Mamaw's washing machine lid was round, could be taken off the ringer type washer, would probably slide like crazy, and Mamaw never had to know. Absolutely, without a doubt, a perfect idea!

After telling the others I'd be right back, I hurried to Mamaw's house. I tiptoed across the front yard, glancing from side to side, and held my breath since my breathing now sounded asthmatic. I heard my own heart beating in the hushed night, though I had yet to commit the dastardly deed.

I crept onto the back porch, careful not to bump into the coal bucket or anything else that would make a noise and draw unwanted attention. (When I grew up, I marveled at the fact the washer remained on the back porch all year long, and its working mechanism never failed to function.)

I lifted the metal lid and nearly fainted when it bumped against the washer. The ding in that silence sounded like a warning bell in my ear. When no one came to discover my theft, I sprinted back across the frozen grass, holding the lid in front of me like a soldier brandishing his shield going into battle.

The laughter that greeted my newest idea sounded like the same laughter I'd heard when my box sled gave up the ghost. I had no idea if it would work or not, but my cousins were certain it would not only *not* work, but if it didn't get me killed Mamaw would finish the job when she found out what I'd done.

I pulled the socks tighter on my hands with a determined jerk. I settled my tail end in the center of the circular lid, gripped the small upturned lip of cold metal, and balanced just on the edge of the precipice. Waiting, rocking back and forth in the frigid breeze, it was as if time itself stood still, waiting to see what that small white washing machine lid would do on the icy surface. I leaned forward ever so slowly, my eyes opened wide and watering from the cold, my fingers so tight on that lid it seemed I'd die with them in that position—and then the delicate balance was taken over by gravity.

It was just like going over the brink of the world's biggest, most exciting, monstrously terrifying roller coaster. The question as to whether or not that lid would slide was answered at the speed of light. That lid ran like a scalded dog! I believed then, as I believe now, I broke the sound barrier in Tulsa, Oklahoma that night!

My hair blew in the wind, my cheeks were pressed back from the G-force, every muscle in my body was tensed from the pure excitement, and my butt was jarred as if riding a wagon over deep ruts along the worst country road. In short, it was utterly fantastic!

When I got to the bottom of the hill, I was so stunned I couldn't move, couldn't breathe, couldn't answer my cousins' questions about the ride. I simply sat there and grinned like the town fool. And that's when it got interesting.

It seemed Mamaw's little washer lid was way better than any shiny new store-bought sled as it spun in rapturous circles like an out-of-control amusement park extravaganza, and every one of my cousins wanted to take it for a spin. Every hurtful, unkind word they'd all said to me about my soggy cardboard box came to mind, and each time one of them *begged* me to ride the lid, I smiled, shook my head, and dropped back to the center of the metal contraption and launched myself back over the precipice. Oh how jealous they were—until Mamaw began to yell.

There, at ten o'clock at night, when all the sensible townsfolk had either gone to bed or were in that general frame of mind, Mae Halsey was shouting, "Gloria Lynn, you come here this very minute!"

I took a quick inventory of everyone who had been there with me, riding the silvered road surface, and saw one face missing. Benny was nowhere in sight, but I knew where he was—in the house, squealing like the pig he was to Mamaw, telling her all about the now scarred, scraped, and dented washing machine lid.

The remaining cousins turned to me with terror in their eyes. They patted me on the back as I shuffled past, lid beneath my arm, making my way down the hill toward decimation. I stopped at the bottom, turned to wave at them for the last time, sniffled so they'd know I was crying, then returned to my journey. My cousins liked to tease me, but none of us liked the way Benny tattled, and this was all the excuse they needed to beat the snot right out of him when he joined them later.

I took as long as possible to open that front door. My grandmother's living room was filled with aunts, uncles, and cousins too old or too embarrassed to go sledding with us. She latched onto my wrist, and I was dragged toward the bedroom by Mamaw's calloused hand. A couple of the adults gave me a gentle swat on my backside, one tousled my hair, but each of them had a look of pity for me when I dared to raise my eyes to look in theirs. This may have been the previous generation, but most, if not all of them, had been "corrected" by Mamaw so they had deep empathy for me.

When Mamaw walked me into the back bedroom and closed the door, I nearly screamed from the pent up fear that others had inspired in my faltering heart.

"Gloria Lynn, you know better than to do what you did. I can't believe you took my washing machine lid and slid down the hill with it! It's so dented and twisted I don't know that it'll ever work again."

"But Mamaw, it's just an old washer lid, not good for nothin'..."

Twin spots of red blossomed on her cheeks and halted any further words from escaping my mouth.

"You listen to me, little girl. It's not your decision to make as to what's good and what isn't, what's worthy and what's without value. When you grow up, you can make up your mind as to what you'll treasure. As for us, for the people in this house, we make the decisions because we pay for everything you have in your life. I know you don't understand, Gloria, but we're poor. We're very poor. We can't afford for you to just take whatever you want, whatever you think is your right to play with or destroy. I cannot afford to replace that lid. Can you? Can you come up with the money to fix that old washer lid, as you call it?"

I mumbled a few unintelligible words, wishing I was anywhere but in that room, alone, with my grandmother.

"What? What did you say, Gloria Lynn? I don't believe I can hear you with your head hanging down so low."

"No Ma'am, I ain't got no money."

"That's right, you don't, so you can't pay to fix the lid or anything else, isn't that right?"

"Yes Ma'am, that's right. I'm so sorry, Mamaw. I didn't mean to ruin your washing machine lid."

"Since you're truly sorry, but yet you have no money, we'll have to think of another way for you to pay for what you've done. Can you think of a suitable punishment, Gloria Lynn?"

"Tell Mommy to make me stay in my room, all by myself, when we get home?"

"Send you to your room with all your toys you love so? That's not punishment and you know it. Good try but it won't work."

"So what are you going to do to me?"

"I'm going to make you wait."

"Make me wait? Wait for what?"

"Wait to see what punishment I come up with. You'll never know when it's going to happen or just how bad it's going to be."

"Oh Lord…"

Mamaw's smile was not one of benevolence.

"Exactly. Now get on out of here before I give you a switchin', too."

Ah, she was a wily one, my grandmother. My life was sheer agony for months after that night. Oh, there were short periods of time when I'd forget about it, but just the right look on her face, one of her sly little winks, and I'd be filled with terror once again that she'd finally hand down my sentence. I had plenty of time to grasp the reality of how much it makes your heart ache to know you've hurt someone you love as much as I loved Mamaw.

The punishment, corporal or otherwise, never came, but the torture of waiting kept me on the straight and narrow path. Mamaw's washing machine lid was forever safe, no matter how deep the snow.

As a girl, Gloria Teague's family told her that her imagination could be her best friend. She's never had any reason to dispute that since it's helped her cope with life's

bumps and bruises. It's even boosted her checking account a few times. She's had dozens of fiction and nonfiction short stories published in national magazines and regional newspapers. Visit her at www.anglefire.com/ok/dreamwvr.

The girl was smiling at me and rubbing the barrette with her fingers. I didn't even know her name.

The Persistence of History
by Sandra Parsons

In the photograph, I'm the one in the backseat, fingers grasping the window frame, stretching my neck so I can see over the edge of the opening, looking at children I didn't know.

We stared silently at each other, trying to figure out why we were different and why it mattered. I was as white-blonde as my dad, and they were what he called "Colored." But I didn't know if that meant their skin or their hair. They seemed as curious about me as I was about them, but none of us would be the first to resolve the cultural standoff we were party to but didn't understand.

It was the 1957 Labor Day weekend, and we had driven from my parents' brick house near the Tulsa Fairgrounds to this little neighborhood near the MKT Railroad tracks for a single purpose: to bootleg. At home, aunts, uncles, and multiple cousins were due for a cookout and the men had conspired to buy a bottle of whiskey to enhance the holiday. Oklahoma was still grasping at the last remnants of the great Prohibition experiment, and hard liquor was illegal, but plentiful, despite colorful and dire admonitions from the pulpit.

I had no idea what bootlegging was but excited that I had managed to cadge a trip in Uncle Walter's new Buick. I scooted from one side of the backseat to the other during the trip, examining the scenery and eavesdropping as my dad and uncle talked. They were drinking beer from sweating brown bottles, chain smoking, and swapping dubious fishing stories.

My uncle was a house painter. A man named Sam worked for him, and he lived at our destination. While my uncle drove, he talked about the stock of whiskey and gin bottles Sam kept behind the house in a storm cellar. I'd been in storm cellars before, hiding from tornadoes, and wrinkled my nose at the thought of keeping anything valuable down there.

We turned off the pavement onto a string of roads that spewed dirt and ugly dogs, and entered a neighborhood of small houses. Sun-baked gardens, old cars, and children were everywhere. A train nearby seemed close enough to touch, and I had to hold my hands over my ears when it whistled. I could smell chicken frying and hear laughter coming from the houses.

When we stopped, Uncle Walter told my dad to get behind the wheel and leave the motor running, because there had been another round of "busts" recently. He said he'd been buying bootleg from Sam for a long time and was going inside to "negotiate," which caused both men to laugh.

So here we were, sitting in the roiling sun with the windows down—waiting.

"Daddy, where are we?"

He was evasive. "We just came to pick up something."

We were in Alsuma, a tiny community southeast of Tulsa's gangly border. Later, it was consumed by the bigger city. It was a hodgepodge collection of houses, sheds, and businesses run out of garages. We were parked next door to a building that looked like it could be a school, but it was only white clapboard and not a big brick building like the one I would be attending.

I got up on my knees on the seat, and stuck my head out the window to look around, trying to comprehend why the streets weren't paved like mine and why there was so little grass. The swirls of hot dust stung my nose and eyes.

"Who are they?" I pointed and asked, wondering if I could go play, which is all a five-year-old wants to do.

"They live here," my father replied, checking the rear-view mirror. He sat behind the steering wheel of the chrome monster with the motor running, despite the searing heat created by the big engine and lack of air conditioning. Music played softly on the AM radio. His fingers tapped to the beat of Porter Waggoner, and my father's customary Chesterfield was between his lips.

"Where's their swing set?" Everyone I knew had a swing set.

"They don't have one."

"Why not? Can I go play?"

"No. Uncle Walter'll be right back."

"Will they go to my school?"

My dad paused and glanced at the laughing children who had resumed riding bicycles and chasing each other in the billows of dust; perhaps he was calculating how much a small girl would understand.

"No, they go to school over there." He gestured toward the clapboard building with the sign I could not yet read—*Alsuma Separate School*.

A boy about ten ran out of the house and approached the car.

"Mister, he wants to know if you want one or two."

"Just one, I think." And the boy was off, slamming the screen door as he re-entered the house.

"One what, Daddy?"

"Something for the grown ups," was the only answer he gave, and I couldn't figure out what else to ask.

The boys began showing off as small boys do, and everyone drifted away from a girl about my age who sat on the school's stoop. I had heard them ask her to join their game, but she shook her head and looked pained as the others walked away. No one stayed to talk to her.

She was better dressed than we were in our wrinkled cotton shorts and shirts. She wore a frilly pink and green dress with a wide ribbon sash, white shoes, and lace-trimmed socks—no one else had on shoes, including me. I thought her hair looked funny, because no girl I knew wore hers like that. She had multiple braids that stuck out all over her head with small barrettes at the ends.

What was most important to me was that she had a book in her hands. We stared at each other. To me she was just another girl my age, even if she looked different.

I made a decision and hung over the front seat to look my dad in the eye. I wanted his full attention.

"Daddy, can I go talk to that girl over there?" I was very determined at five.

My dad swung his head over to look at the girl, checked where all the other kids were—scanned the rearview mirror again, looking for something unknown—and back to look at me. I could tell he was hesitant, but I didn't know why.

"You come when I call you," he said, and I gleefully jumped back to open the door.

I approached the girl with all the confidence and innocent bravado I had, sat down next to her, and asked, "What's in the book?"

"Pictures of baby animals," she said, and opened the worn covers of the Golden Book to show me. "My mama's teaching me to read."

We sat side-by-side as she turned each page of the small book, touching the colorful drawings of the animals and imitating their sounds. We were giggling well before getting to "S is for Snake" where we said "Yuck!" in unison.

"Why aren't you playing with the other kids?" I asked.

"Mama told me not to get dirty. We're going to something at church." She unconsciously reached down to smooth her skirt.

I looked her over as if I was trying to help her keep clean and reached across to gently remove a speck of dirt from her face.

"We both have pink barrettes," I said.

Her face was a moue as she showed me a braid with a small rubber band on the end and no barrette.

"Yeah, but I lost one."

We returned to the book for a few minutes before Uncle Walter came out of the house with another man. They were laughing loudly, and Uncle Walter was thanking him for "the samples" as he waved and approached the Buick. He carried a brown paper sack and boasted, "I got two—they were small," to my laughing father.

I heard my name, and my dad stepped out to open the car's back door.

"Here, you can have this one," I said as I removed a barrette from my hair and gave it to her.

I ran back to the car and jumped inside before he could call me again. Daddy put it in reverse and started for home as I waved out the window. The girl was smiling at me and rubbing the barrette with her fingers. I didn't even know her name.

We went home, and the trip to Alsuma became just another memory of growing up in Tulsa. Nothing big, nothing important; just a childhood memory for more than fifty years, I thought, looking at a black-and-white photograph of my father and me sitting in that big Buick.

I was stunned. I had come to a Centennial exhibit of historical Tulsa photographs and had discovered that I was part of the display. Where had this photo come from?

Soon I found another one of me sitting on the stoop of the Alsuma Separate School. I was the "unidentified young girl" sharing the Golden Book, but she had a name—Ardetta Perry. There were a few others from Alsuma that had been originally printed in the *Oklahoma Eagle*, but they were just a tiny portion of the exhibit. I even found another one of Ardetta in her twenties, singing with Ernie C. Fields, Sr.'s band at an after-hours club off Greenwood. I smiled, remembering how much I had enjoyed visiting those clubs and dancing to local jazz groups.

I had been gone from Tulsa for more than three decades, returning for family visits when I could, but I'd recently returned permanently. The photos brought back happy memories of places and things that I had grown up with, and they were helping me reacquaint myself with my hometown.

When I left the exhibit, I vowed to act like a tourist and roam the streets to see the art deco buildings, old houses, museums, and whatever else would help me rebuild a sense of place. And, I thought, Alsuma might be a good place to start.

Several weeks after visiting the photography exhibit, I took the sketchy information I'd found on the Internet and got in my car to find what was left of Alsuma. As a child, the drive had seemed long—way out in the countryside. I was surprised to discover the old neighborhood was only two miles east of the population center of Tulsa, buried up against the convergence of two major highways.

I turned off Mingo Road and drove into a mix of commercial buildings and storage facilities. There were few homes, and those mostly housed small home service businesses. The creek had been channeled dry, and soccer fields covered a wide expanse where homes previously stood.

I parked next to the only building old enough to be part of what I remembered. It was white clapboard, supported by unstable looking concrete blocks. The boarded-over doors were in the wrong places, and there was no stoop, so it wasn't the school where Ardetta and I sat with her book. The post office had closed long ago, as had the railroad station. The little community had disappeared into history.

With the remnants of Alsuma in my rearview mirror, I mentally inventoried all the other parts of my Tulsa childhood that had disappeared in the decades since, but didn't dwell on the losses. Progress changes everything, tearing down and paving over what is no longer valuable in its present form—people remain the only constant.

Alsuma and Ardetta were gone, but not from my memories.

Sandra Parsons recently turned to fiction writing after many years as a successful business and research writer. She has a long list of publications to her credit, but admits that academic journals have never made the best seller lists. She returned to Tulsa in 2006 after being away for more than 25 years. She continues to contract in the business world while completing her first mystery and a series of short stories.

In Vandevers, one of the owners manned the elevator from time to time.

Oil Deals and Window Shopping in the 1930's
by Sue Forney

It was always a treat to go to Tulsa. Back in the 30's when I was a little girl, we lived in a small Oklahoma town. Mother and I would go to Tulsa with my father when he wanted to talk about "oil deals."

A lot of deals were made in Tulsa hotel lobbies back then. Men who didn't have offices of their own would meet there to talk about what wells were being drilled or were going to be drilled and who had leases on nearby property. A lease on land near a well that struck oil could be very valuable.

A favorite hotel where oil deals were made was the Ketchum on Main Street. Once in a while one of the "big boys" in the oil business, like Bill Skelly, would show up to see what leases somebody had to offer. The lobby was often heavy with cigar smoke as the men huddled over maps of Oklahoma counties and leases. While all of this "oil talk" was going on, Mother and I would be free to "look around town."

It was fun to look in the windows of the stores on Main Street. The windows were dressed by people who knew how to display what the stores offered. We saw I. Miller Shoes, Streets, Fields, Seidenbachs, Clarks, and department stores like Vandevers and Brown-Dunkin. Most of these stores were locally owned, not affiliated with chain stores. In Vandevers, one of the owners manned the elevator from time to time. Elevators in department stores stopped at each floor, and the operator called out what was offered on that floor, "Fourth floor: Children's Wear and Lingerie."

Usually, Mother and I didn't buy anything, but we had a great time looking at all the things you could find in Tulsa. We met my father for dinner, usually at Michaelis Cafeteria, across the street from Sears & Roebuck, and, afterwards, we might see a movie at either the Orpheum or the Ritz.

All of these places are only memories now. They are part of an earlier time in a great town, Tulsa.

Sue Forney is a retired teacher/counselor with Tulsa Public Schools. She has lived in Tulsa for most of her 82 years.

*Being an usher at a Ralph Talbot theater was a highly prized
job. You had to be the right size, shape, and age to apply.*

Reflections on the Tulsa Coliseum, Ritz
Theater, Organs, and Organists
by Bill Forney

My memories of the Tulsa Coliseum started early, but they
were especially memorable in my teens. We ice skated there for
years accompanied by Clarence Wood at the organ. The one-
story building covered a city block at 11th and Denver streets in
Tulsa. Most large gatherings, graduations, basketball games,
rodeos, conventions, public ice skating, and hockey games took
place there. Unfortunately, a fire destroyed it on September 21,
1952. One man who lived close to the Coliseum was quoted as
saying, "I saw a blinding lightning flash immediately before the
fire started." In fact, the fire was thought to have been started by
lightning.

The Coliseum wasn't the only venue that occupied my
thoughts as a young man. Movies were very popular. In 1938
and 1939, the center of Tulsa was the intersection of 4th and
Main Street, and near this center were the four largest movie
theaters in town. These Ralph Talbot Theaters were named the
Ritz, Orpheum, Majestic, and Rialto. The Ritz was the most
elegant and beautiful. Its lower floor seated about a thousand
people and the balcony about 500. At the balcony level, loge
seats were located at the sides of the theater close to the stage.
The ceiling was painted a dark blue. Pinpoint lights in the ceiling
blinked like stars. The seats were deep, soft, and adjustable. No
food or drink, not even popcorn, was sold or even permitted
inside the building. Two aisles divided both the ground floor and
the balcony, and a uniformed usher waited at the entrance of
each aisle with a small flashlight to guide patrons to their seats.

Being an usher at a Ralph Talbot theater was a highly prized
job. You had to be the right size, shape, and age to apply.
Fortunately, I was 6' 2", skinny, and a high school student. I was
hired to usher every weekday evening from five p.m. until
closing, usually around midnight. On weekends I worked from
opening time, about noon, to closing.

Each usher's uniform was tailored for him. It consisted of a short Eton jacket and a pair of pants without pockets. Instead of a shirt, we wore a white, starched dickey front with a collar and a black bow tie. The usher manager was Bud Patton, a natty dresser who had his suits tailored as well. The ushers all admired him. He taught us how to stand, to walk, and how to glide smoothly up and down stairs instead of bouncing or staggering.

We stood at our assigned position in a stance similar to a military Parade Rest. Our feet far apart and our hands clasped together in front, we had to stand for prolonged periods in that position without moving. During especially long movies, we learned to lock our muscles and yet relax into semi-sleep until approached by a patron.

When a special movie or other performance was scheduled, a line of people formed outside the theater. Sometimes the line was more than two blocks long wrapping around three sides of the buildings without crossing a street.

Many shows were two hours long, and on weekends, the last feature always started at 9:30. Depending on running time, we closed at 11:30 or 12:30 p.m. To figure when we had to be at work, ushers counted backward from 9:30.

I lived in Red Fork, which was 10 miles from the Ritz Theater. Streetcars ran from Red Fork to Tulsa, but not after midnight. If closing ran late, I had a tough time getting home. Earlier in the evening, I could hitchhike, but there was little traffic past twelve a.m. Sometimes I walked the ten miles home, and I didn't look forward to it after standing at attention all day.

One day I arrived at work early. The front door was unlocked, but the ushers' dressing room was locked. I heard organ music. The instrument was in the orchestra pit—the lowest part of the theater. I walked to the back row of seats in the balcony, the highest place to sit in the dark theater. The "stars" in the ceiling guided me. Far below, faint lights on the keyboard revealed the organist at practice. The organist, Milton Slosser, had turned up the volume, and the entire theater reverberated with classical music. That day, he and I were the only people in the theater. It stirred emotions I have never forgotten. I can still picture the simulated sky and twinkling stars, the faint light of the organ far below, and the huge empty theater filled with music.

Years later, I searched for information about the Ritz organist, Milton Slosser, and the Coliseum organist, Clarence Wood. I talked to Phil Judkins, past president of the Sooner State Chapter of the American Theater Organ Society. He knew and remembered both men. Phil recounted his own memorable experience of organ music. At age three, his brother took him to the Ritz Theater to hear Milton Slosser play. The experience started him on a lifelong practice of working with organs and organ players. During that period before television, organ music was highly appreciated.

Phil Judkins, recalled that Clarence Wood and Milton Slosser rigged up a connection where they could hear each other on earphones as they played their respective organs at the Ritz and the Coliseum, and they played duets. The music was mixed at KVOO Studios by radio engineer Harry Rasmussen and was broadcast over KVOO Radio. Phil says he never heard of such a unique radio broadcast before or since. Although Milton Slosser and Clarence Wood are no longer with us, I'll always remember the emotionally moving moments they gave me in my youth.

Bill Forney is 86 years young and spends time on the tennis court almost every day. A retired mechanical engineer, Bill has lived most of his life in Tulsa.

He was more independent than some of "the powers that be" really liked; they didn't want change, and he was bringing change.

Memories of a District Attorney: Commercial Gambling on Main Street
by James D. Jordan

In 1979, there was an open gambling hall in the front of a business building one block away from the Creek Council House. It was less than two blocks from the County Courthouse on Main Street in Okmulgee, Oklahoma. Gambling was illegal. If gambling was going on within his district, a district attorney was presumed under the law to know about it. He could be removed from office for not actively prosecuting such gaming.

Austin O. Webb had served as County Attorney and then District Attorney for Okmulgee and McIntosh Counties longer than any other prosecutor in the state of Oklahoma. There were people who wanted Webb out of office, but it seemed clear that whoever took the challenge would face a rough and tumble fight. James D. Jordan ran on his own without any group of organized supporters, just appealing to the people. Support grew as the race was under way, and he won—not owing a thing to any group or any politician. He was more independent than some of "the powers that be" really liked; they didn't want change, and he was bringing change. Now that Webb was out of office, Jordan had to walk a narrow line and follow the law; otherwise, he would have found *himself* out of office. It was imperative to prosecute illegal gambling.

But the practical problem was that a few prominent people in Okmulgee were active customers of this gambling establishment. The chief of police wanted to keep his job and not upset the powerful locals who could impact how long he served. The duty of the chief of police was basically to preserve peace and safety in the community, but the statutory pressure was on the district attorney.

The solution was to call in Drew Diamond from the Tulsa Police Department to run the operation. This was before Diamond became Chief of Police for Tulsa. When it was time for the raid, District Attorney Jordan was called to the police station. The street officers who were to participate in the raid were locked in a room. Jordan was ushered into the same locked room and remained there until the raid was underway. Apparently, none of the officers wanted to take the blame and have Jordan claim the raid was strictly a police matter and that he had no involvement. By staying in the locked room with the officers, the D.A. insured that he, as well as the police, shared political blame for the raid.

This action of the D.A., staying in the locked room until the end of the raid, helped to build trust and confidence between the police officers and the district attorney. The assignment was given in the locked room, and prior to leaving, one of the officers commented that a single phone call right then would be worth $3,000. This comment was taken as a joke by everyone there. But it probably was true.

The walls of the gambling hall appeared to be plastered cement. There was nothing but a pay phone on the east wall. A ragged chunk of plaster about the size of an orange was missing from the wall next to the phone. One of the officers pointed out that the hole had been made by a gun fired from the direction of the bar long before the raid. Apparently it was left as a warning to dissatisfied customers, "Don't call the police."

After the raid, the gambling hall operator was charged with a felony. The players were charged in city court, allowed to post bond and plead nolo contendere, and forfeit their bond as their total punishment. At the time of trial, each gambler was called to testify and had difficulty remembering that he was even there, much less that any one of them was involved in gambling. Their memory was refreshed when the records were presented in open court clearly showing the presence, arrest, and forfeiture of bond by each player. The jury had no problem understanding the facts of the case and reaching what the twelve members felt was a just verdict.

The District Attorney had done his job.

One more day in the life of an Oklahoma District Attorney, serving justice.

Tulsa author and retired United States Administrative Law Judge James D. Jordan was elected to serve as District

Attorney for Okmulgee and McIntosh counties and took office January 1, 1979.

I would take home the icon along with the ceramic mirror and have it appraised sometime way down the road.

Antiques No-Show
by Jill Byrne

"There is only one thing in this house that may be of real value, and if anything should ever happen to me, I want you to have it." My sister Beverly said these words to me a few years before something did happen to her. She died suddenly in August, 1999.

Seven years earlier a friend of means had presented Beverly with a 17th century Russian icon after returning from a stay in the Ukraine. Beverly displayed it in her den, hung just below an old mirror encased in ceramic brown lattice with green ivy. To my untrained eye the ceramic mirror appeared the work of a rank beginner.

On the other hand, it was evident the icon had once been a work of exquisite beauty. Placed on a slightly bowed panel of wood, roughly 9"x12", were three figures done in intricate patterns of copper and tin. The frayed halos curled away from the board highlighting the delicate faces painted on the wood. Everything about it spelled A-N-T-I-Q-U-E.

After a discussion with Blake, Beverly's son and executor, we concurred. I would take home the icon along with the ceramic mirror and have it appraised sometime way down the road. The road shortened considerably six months later when it was announced that the Antiques Roadshow would be coming to Tulsa in mid-summer. Tickets would be available at noon on the Saturday of Memorial Day weekend. Most of my friends made plans for the lake or other destinations for the holiday. I, however, felt called to take advantage of this unexpected opportunity for a free appraisal. At twelve sharp I dialed, prepared to speak with someone associated with the show. When a recording answered, I panicked and hung up the phone. I quickly regrouped and tried again and again for the next hour with no success. Though I had never ordered anything over the Internet, desperation forced me to give it a try. The next day I read where all tickets were gone in an hour and a half. A few weeks later I was shocked when four tickets arrived in the mail, but I took it as a clear sign I was moving in the right direction.

Judiciously dispensing my three remaining tickets, I gave one to my neighbor and friend, Carolyn, and we made plans to go together. Several friends came to view my treasure, and I cautioned *all* not to get *too* close. The frayed metal appeared fragile, and the oil from our skin might somehow tarnish and cause further deterioration. Carolyn's daughter also came. As president of a local antique club, she was duly impressed and asked if I had any other antiques. I brought out that old mirror which she immediately identified as Majolica. She insisted I take it along for a professional look-see as well.

The upcoming show was a frequent topic of conversation with general agreement that there were fewer centuries-old antiques per capita in our young state compared to areas back East. So as the time neared, my confidence in being discovered soared. Beverly's icon, and possibly the mirror, would surely catch the eyes of highly skilled appraisers, probably setting me apart from run of the mill collectors.

With no hesitation, I acquiesced when advised by a friend to forego my casual attire of jeans, tee shirt, and tennies and really spruce up in something nice. Our tickets had a specific start time of twelve noon, which gave me time to have my hair done, don my chocolate brown, brushed silk pantsuit and black flats, bolt down a light lunch, and pack a small cosmetic bag for the green room. When Carolyn picked me up, the icon was already packed in a borrowed ice chest that I strapped to a dolly while the mirror was secure in a small rolling flight bag.

As my momentum built, I alerted Beverly's three children that good fortune was just around the corner. Should the icon exceed five digits in value I would call each from the floor of the convention center to confer about an instant college fund for Beverly's six grandchildren.

Once inside the Tulsa Convention Center, Carolyn and I rolled our treasures in a constantly moving line for the next three hours. Shortly after three o'clock we parted to await the moments of discovery in our respective areas. Forgotten were my tired legs and sore feet as I gingerly unveiled the icon and placed it in the appraiser's hands. I stepped back with baited breath ready to capture his "Ah-ha" moment as he realized the significance of such a rare find. While still bent over the wood, he motioned me nearer. "Do you see these small holes around the edge?" he asked. "Yes." I said, nearly bursting with pride. "Obviously the frame that was ripped away was worth much more than the icon itself, still I suspect you could get one or two hundred dollars for it." His voice faded away as he turned to the next person in line. With a gentle Frisbee flick of the wrist, I returned the icon to the ice chest and trudged on to the Majolica area. That guesstimate was three times the value of the icon, but no consolation. The dream of college for six was dashed with the reality of insufficient funds for a week of summer camp for one.

I hope Beverly enjoyed the irony as her little sister shuffled off for a margarita on a hot summer Saturday—wearing her Sunday best.

Jill Byrne's recently completed memoir, _And Jill Came Tumbling After_, is now awaiting publication. A native Oklahoman and long-time Tulsan, Jill is eager to share her story of recovery from a lifetime of depression. Founder of a successful "Senior" line of occasion cards called Magshots, dressed-up greeting cards; she enjoys a good perm from time to time. Jill invites you to learn more at www.jillbyrne.com.

After all these years, she could still remember the sense of foreboding that had trickled down her spine.

Progression of Life
by Bren Rothrock Presley

The towering steeple of Asbury Methodist Church overshadowed most of the places Katie Mae Kirk's life had developed. She stood beside the green-black Mercedes fighting back tears. The large imposing building of Mathis Brothers Furniture invaded the sky, obliterating anything familiar around the area where her grandparent's home once stood. What had been soft hay fields were now hard concrete, the green pastureland had turned to black asphalt, and shade trees were replaced by shopping malls. Taking a slow turn, Katie searched for something familiar, some semblance of where her early memories were born. Her home.

Surely, she thought, there is something left, and why do I care? Toward the northwest was an overgrown muddy area where an old gnarled tree stood beckoning. Katie hastened toward it with no concern whether she damaged her expensive pumps. The old oak was tall with one or two branches seeming to strain for the stars. Many of the branches bent in unusual angles, and it was evident that storms and bulldozers had not honored the old tree. Reaching out to touch the rough bark, she was overwhelmed with sadness and began to sob, wrapping her arms around the aged anchor for support. Slowly, the sound and smell of memories washed over her.

A motorcycle sped by, rousing her. She stumbled back toward her car and the paved four-lane street. As she stood staring at the lights reflected in the street's blackness, Katie recalled a time more than sixty years earlier.

At five years of age, she had stood beside the same road, barefoot, staring at oil splattered gravel. She was plotting a way to cross without having to step on the oil because Mama scrubbed the bottoms of small feet with Ajax to get them clean. That hurt! The destination was the flour-soft dirt of her Granny and Grandpa's drive. She made up her mind and darted across to the cool dirt.

71

Dressed in a starched and ironed gingham dress with a half torn waistline, sashes undone and dragging on the ground, Katie marched toward her grandparents. She had just been scolded harshly, once again, by Mama for damaging another dress. But Granny would understand that a small girl was often too busy playing and she sometimes forgot and stepped on her sash tails.

Clenched in her small fist was the handle of a doll suitcase that contained the necessary items she needed to stay with Granny. Held tightly under one arm, a dirty, child-sized quilt and clothes for a doll were all she needed. She ran up the drive, scooting her feet along in the dirt to produce a smoke trail behind an imaginary car.

"Granny," Katie had called from the honeysuckle-covered gate, "where are you? Can I stay? I brought my suitcase." Turning and pointing across the road, she had demanded, "Let's 'tend we don't know who lives over there. Okay?"

Her grandmother had come chuckling onto the porch, drying her hands on the ever-present apron. "I reckon. What you done now?" Granny had asked with love and welcome evident in her voice.

As the memory faded a soft smile appeared on the face of the now grown five-year-old. Even after six decades, she could still smell the starch from her grandmother's ironing, the fragrance of snickerdoodles in the oven, and the tang of Grandpa's tobacco. Why must life go by so fast? Why can't it all be grannies and snickerdoodles? Then another memory made her frown.

A confident, eighteen-year-old Katie stood fidgeting while her mama pinned the back of a just-sewn wedding dress. As she looked at the silhouette in the mirror, she was suddenly afraid. The image was mesmerizing and shocking the way the wedding dress seemed to change her. The white lace and satin made her different, beautiful, and yet unsure. Without warning, she twirled around.

"I'll be right back!" Picking up the long train basted to the empire waist, she had run barefoot across that same gravel road, down the dusty drive, and onto her grandparent's porch.

"Granny," she called, "come look at my dress."

"You're too damn young to get married," responded a gruff voice. Then, a choked, "Don't do it. Not yet. Just wait, ya' got plenty of time." Turning, startled by the speaker, Katie realized Grandpa had been sitting under a shade tree beside the porch. Without further comment, he'd picked up his cane, stalked to his car, and sped off.

After all these years, she could still remember the sense of foreboding that had trickled down her spine. Uncertainty and fear made her want to run after him, do as he said, and call off the wedding. Yet, as Granny's voice came from the screen door, Katie could remember shaking off the unease. Seven short years later—after a painful divorce—she had wished she'd paid attention to the premonition.

Thoughts and memories came from all directions—remembrances so strong of joyous births and painful deaths. Each family member died one after another, even her mother and sister in the same year. Now she, like the old tree, was the only one left. Her eyes and demeanor reflected the tragic times she had endured, times when she'd faced storms and bulldozers that had almost destroyed her. Undeterred by sadness and sorrow, she had continued reaching for the stars.

Katie stood tall and straightened her shoulders. The sounds and smells that invaded her senses today were very different from those of childhood. Traffic, thumping stereos, and construction noises replaced locusts, crickets, and children's laughter. Looking once more at the navy blue sky and the early stars, she felt a smile form. It led to a contented feeling of appreciation for the years she had lived in this place. Closing her eyes and taking a deep breath, they were there again. Memories, oh the memories—of tragedy and triumph, sorrow and sunshine. She felt a renewed determination to claim every ounce of happiness in the years ahead.

After one last glance around, she hurried to the car. The regret and aching grief that had been a part of her life for so long were fading at last. This visit had reassured her that, although nothing was left, it was all still there.

Starting the car, happiness growing in her heart, she drove toward the rest of her life.

Bren Presley is from Wagoner, Oklahoma and teaches 6th grade Language Arts in Muskogee. A recent widow, Brenda is currently writing about the reality of losing a spouse. She has been writing most of her adult life. When she isn't writing, she spends time with her four grandchildren.

I tried not to think about the friends and family we'd hugged in our final tearful goodbyes.

A Nod in the Right Direction
by Carla Stewart

I zipped the packing tape on another box and straightened, wiping the sweat from my forehead with one hand and reaching for the Magic Marker with the other. *Photos. Graduation stuff.* I scribbled and hefted the box atop the one labeled *FFA*. One more, and then it was time for a break. Stiff, grimy, and weary, I picked out a book box from the stack against the wall and assembled it. When would it ever end?

The golden glow of late afternoon filtered through the fringed curtains, projecting distorted rectangles on the bare walls. A lump clogged my throat. Eleven years in this old house, and now we were casting it all off, moving clear across the state. *Tulsa.* Whatever possessed us to sell the family farm? Max's grandfather crafted this house more than sixty years ago. Now, we'd gone and sold out. Would the new owners take care of it? Would they appreciate the history, the toil of human hands that went into making the house a home?

Still, we'd made our decision. Max had a new job, and our youngest son would soon be off to college. The opportunity we'd prayed for had become a reality. In six days, we would load the truck and wave goodbye to some of the best years of our lives.

The ache in my arms didn't compare to the heaviness that burrowed into my chest. *Would people come and visit us? Would we find a church? Friends?* Kicking aside the box I should have been filling with more stuff, I wove my way through the waist-high maze of those already filled and went to the kitchen. I swallowed two Tylenol while water heated in the microwave for a cup of tea. Then I gazed out the kitchen window at the endless miles of prairie grass and wheat fields. My breath caught as a string of blue quail strutted single file beneath a row of Russian olive trees we'd planted when we first came to live on the farm.

When the microwave beeped, I plunked a tea bag in my cup and headed for the front door. A bundle of black fur whipped

75

around the porch's concrete pillar and bounded up the steps to greet me.

"Hi, Buddy. Care for a cuppa?" After patting the dog on the head, I slumped into the metal rocker, sticking my feet up on the low wall of the porch. *Yes!* The muscles in my back relaxed in the soft breeze of dusk. My favorite time of day. I leaned back and enjoyed the quiet.

Bwak! A ring-neck pheasant fluttered up from the culvert down the drive. Iridescent gold and crimson feathers caught the light as the bird glided across the landscape and stole the breath right out of me. Now that's a sight I wouldn't be privy to in Tulsa.

Buddy squirmed beside me and began to whimper. *He knows something is up.* And sadly, our move to the city didn't include taking Buddy. He, too, would have a new home. I swallowed the lump in my throat and looked up. Coming up our long driveway was a white-tailed doe. She ambled along, picking her way among the ruts in the road, so nonchalant and sure-footed. Oh my.

When she sees me, she'll bolt.

As I kept my eyes on the doe, she crept nearer, and every few feet she stopped and raised her head, sniffing the air. *She'll smell us and run away.* Buddy whimpered again, but he stayed put as my steady hand stroked his thick fur. Even through his massive coat, my fingers sensed his taut muscles, ready to spring into action.

Motionless, I watched as the deer inched closer and closer, until she was only fifty or sixty feet away. I held my breath when she lifted her head and looked straight at me. Eye to eye. *This is it. Now she'll run.* Instead, she kept her gaze locked on mine. In the evening's golden gray, time was suspended. Never in the years we'd lived here had a deer come so near the yard. Why, now?

After what seemed like an eternity, the doe stretched her head even further up and gave a couple of quick nods. A greeting? Acknowledgement that I was there? Just the two nods. Then, gracefully, she lowered her head and continued her walk past the garage and out of sight.

Everything's going to be okay, she'd seemed to say with the nod of her head.

Would it?

I didn't know the answer, but a calm I hadn't felt in many days washed over me. The task at hand didn't seem so daunting anymore. The glow of the twilight encounter energized me, and I got right back to work packing boxes.

A few days later, the moving truck came, and transplanted us onto a meandering, tree-lined street in south Tulsa—a lovely neighborhood of older homes. As luck would have it, heavy rains and a ruthless heat wave descended on the city that same week. Not even a breath of air stirred to bring a respite from the death-defying humidity. Some welcome.

This is my new home. I tried to convince myself, even though everything felt curiously different and out of place. It didn't feel like home, just a nice house, ready to take on the identity of its new owners—us. And that wouldn't happen unless I got busy. Throwing myself into unpacking, I tried not to think about the friends and family we'd hugged in our final tearful goodbyes.

Dripping with perspiration after a full day of emptying boxes, I grabbed a bottle of water and retreated to our covered patio. Maybe, just maybe, a gust of cool air would happen along.

I sat in the porch rocker we'd brought from the farm and took a long drink. No breeze to cool my face. No horizon to set my sights on. As the refreshing water trickled down my throat, my eyes drifted to the tall sycamore tree in our backyard. I craned my neck to see the top. Huge broad leaves and arching branches made a canopy of shade. Then, bursting from the uppermost limbs, two squirrels barreled down the trunk. Around and around, they chased each other, their bushy tails flitting here and there.

From the corner of my eye, I saw a pair of turtledoves light on the fence, their cooing love song filling the air. Other birds, tiny brown ones with red underbellies, swooped in and around the patio, chirping and flapping their feathers. I chuckled, and that's when I spotted a half-grown cottontail nibbling tender blades of grass a few feet away. It was like the welcome wagon, complete with music, right here in my own backyard. There were critters everywhere, scampering, munching, chattering.

As I leaned back and enjoyed the moment, a whisper of a breeze kicked up and rustled the leaves overhead.

The patio door swung open, and Max stepped out with a foil-covered pan in his hand.

"A gal from across the street brought this. She'll come by to visit later when we have time."

A note atop the foil read, "Welcome to the neighborhood." When I peeked inside the pan, the smell of chocolate wafted toward me. Homemade brownies fresh from the oven. We helped ourselves to the melt-in-your-mouth goodness from our neighbor as I quizzed Max about who she was. Did she seem nice? How old? Would she be my first friend in our new home? Somehow, I thought she would. The weariness lifted.

The doe had been right. Everything *was* going to be okay. Somehow God's creation and nice folks had made their way to the heart of the city. Living in Tulsa was going to be fine. Just fine.

Carla Stewart writes creative non-fiction and novels. She is active in many writers' organizations and was one of fifteen chosen to attend the 2002 Guideposts Writers Workshop in Rye, NY. Her stories have appeared in *Guideposts*, *Angels on Earth*, *Saddle Baron: Magazine of the West*, and *Blood and Thunder: Musings on the Art of Medicine*. You can visit her at her website www.carlastewart.com.

He loved the way that dumpster kicked back, that rusty dumpster sound against the boy-blue tricycle sound. The red blood was incidental...

Rocket Grief
by Paula Watkins Alfred

"I know the exact day when I lost my mind." This is what Tom said to her, her father, whom she still called "Daddy" in the Southern way, despite her forty-five years. Good taste said she should have called him father, and at the very least, dad. She never gave it a thought until she heard herself tell a coworker that her daddy was having some trouble. Tennie felt embarrassed she still used that word, which felt both right and obscene at the same time. Maybe it was the fact she was a criminal defense lawyer in big-city Tulsa, not the country child in Fanshawe, Oklahoma, that made it feel obscene. Maybe it was nothing more than her coworker's look of astonishment over Tennie's use of the salad fork rather than the dinner fork at the sit-down-dinner law firm. But that was then.

Now, now she was at her parents' house, their home of thirty years, so Daddy felt right once again. Tennie sat in the porch swing. She could hear happy sounds from the nearby Tulsa fairgrounds. Daddy sat in a patio chair directly across from her. She looked into his Paul Newman blue eyes, vivid against his burnished summer tan and short sandy hair. She felt tears she would not cry in the soles of her feet, which pushed hard against the concrete of her parents' patio. Ruby, Tennie's mom, was playing with the grandkids out of hearing distance. Daddy sat waiting for her response like Tennie used to wait for his words, because his words meant the most. She didn't know why, only that they did. A word of praise from Daddy was worth ten from her mom. His words, scarce and infrequent, felt solid like hardwood. In his youth, Daddy was the Tulsa Driller, strong, stern, unbendable, always the same.

The hot concrete burned her bare feet, but otherwise time had stopped, stopped her breath, stopped her heart, and stopped her mouth. Her mind and heart perched on the end of the high diving board. On the brink of falling, she looked back, but she

79

knew the ladder behind her had been removed. The dive inevitable, but still she delayed. A child's laughter took over the silence, chimes tinkling in the wind. Tennie's attention rushed toward the reprieve of the new sound.

They both watched—she and Daddy. They watched Dillon, the only grandson, low in the tricycle saddle, leaning forward as if to tell the back wheels they needed to catch up. He sped as fast as he could toward the trash dumpster, aiming for Tulsa Talks Trash stenciled on the side, the dumpster rented by a neighbor knee deep in renovation. Dillon careened into the dumpster at full speed just as Ruby yelled, "Dillon."

Tennie recognized love on Dillon's face in that crashing moment. He loved the way the dumpster kicked back, that rusty dumpster sound against the boy-blue tricycle sound. The red blood was incidental, nothing Dillon wouldn't gladly give again, if offered one more chance.

Tennie remembered Christmas when she was three, or maybe she was four. Nothing could ever surprise her in quite the same way as the red tricycle Santa had left under the tree. Well, maybe cancer would have the same shock value, but who wants that?

Tennie and Mae, her older sister, ran to the living room that morning at full speed. Mae with her longer legs got there first. When Tennie burst into the room, she caught sight of the tricycle. It was a quick, "I can't believe it," look that didn't last much longer than the flash of Ruby's camera when she took a picture with the box she called Brownie. Tennie stopped, closed her eyes then opened them again to make sure it was real.

As she approached the tricycle, she could taste the candy-apple-red-fun of the handlebars. Her fingers fondled the red and white streamers that dangled from the handles just like Aunt Nell's Christmas earrings dangled from her ears. Tennie could picture their red and white streamers extended by the wind. She felt the slick plastic speed of them, and her heart screamed, fast, fast, faster. Her nostrils opened wider to take in the new tire smell, blacker than licorice. She palmed the tires letting them roll on the road of her hands. But the absolute best part was the silver spokes that turned as she pushed the tricycle out from under the tree.

She climbed on carefully, not sure how it would feel to sit in the perfect white seat. It felt just right! When she lifted her nightgown and placed her bare feet on the pedals, the push sent chills down her spine all the way to her toes. Go, go, go, yelled her feet! Who could resist their call? It looked deceivingly easy, this peddling and guiding the handlebars at the same time. She crashed into the presents under the tree.

Ruby, her mom, cried, "Careful, Tennie Jane." Tennie looked at Ruby. It was a softer *be careful* than when she was about to spill milk on Ruby's clean floors. When her front tire accidentally hit the Christmas tree shaking the big red tree lights, the whole world felt wobbly, the same wobbly red world as when she turned in a circle as fast as she could, counting all the way to a hundred.

Her parents beamed as if they were the ones who had come up with this gift beyond words, but Tennie knew it was Santa. She looked to see if Santa had eaten the piece of pumpkin pie she and Mae had left on the kitchen table, along with a big glass of milk.

"He ate it!" Tennie sang as she danced around her tricycle. Only then did she notice that Mae had gotten a bicycle. Mae's bike was as blue as ink and as silver as stars. Tennie paused to watch Mae. Mae couldn't take her eyes off the bicycle, but she could not touch it. Too, too, beautiful.

"Okay girls. No riding in the house." Ruby began handing out the unopened packages putting them in stacks close to Tennie or Mae. Daddy sat in the corner dipping Skoal, spitting the brown tobacco juice into the old coffee can. Not quite a part of things, Daddy was the trim, the fringe on Tennie's favorite skirt.

Ruby made the girls eat Christmas dinner before they were allowed to take their new gifts outside. Daddy pulled the pickup close to the house so they could ride back and forth on the black dirt driveway.

"Tennie, remember not to leave your tricycle behind the pickup. Someone will run over it?" Ruby asked it like a question to be sure that Tennie heard her.

"I won't forget, Mom. I won't forget." Tennie yelled at the top of her lungs as she trailed behind Mae to the very edge of the street where their world stopped.

It was later that day when the whole family was in the pickup. They were going to see Grandpa Ed and Grandma Lewis. The engine started just like always, but as the pickup went backward Tennie heard her tricycle make its death cry. The cry started in the bumper, made its way through the bed of the truck, entered the back of the seat, and forced its way into Tennie's throat where it sat like a rock too big too move. LOUD, LOUDER, LOUDEST! Then silence, quiet as a falling star and just as wishful.

The whole family got out of the pickup careful not to touch each other. Tennie closed her eyes. She was afraid to look, just like she was afraid to look at Great Grandpa Hooper lying in that gray casket last summer in the church at Fanshawe, as if not looking could bring a person or a tricycle back to life. Ruby's deep sigh lifted Tennie's eyelids against her will. Her tricycle was dead. Dead before she could even give it a name. She hadn't been able to decide between Rocket, Bullet, or maybe even Rowdy, her favorite Rawhide character. Her tricycle was dead as a dog on the side of the road. Halved in two just like a fold-over peanut butter and jelly sandwich. The red streaks on the silver pickup bumper looked like blood.

"What did we tell you, Tennie?" Daddy looked at her in his stern way that hid the heartbreak he must have been feeling. Stern, to cover what could not be said to a child, that Santa would not bring another because he had spent all the money he had.

"I'm so sorry, Daddy. I forgot." The tears sputtered from her effort not to let them fall. She had no breath.

Daddy kicked the tricycle out from under the bumper, but there was no life left in the sound. They got back in the pickup, Tennie in between Mae and Ruby. Ruby's arm around her. Mae's hand on her knee. Pat, pat, pat. Daddy drove all the way to Grandma's looking out the driver's side of the window, face hidden.

The family grieved all the next day, all the next week, until only Tennie's grief was left, small and tight, in the very center of the palms of her hand.

Daddy smiled as if Dillon had been sharing a joke between him and Tennie. "It was the day I painted the cellar. I shouldn't have done it, should I? The fumes and all. Haven't been the same since."

It was as good an explanation of Alzheimer's as Tennie had ever heard. It sounded like metal against metal, the sound of Rocket dying on a sunny Christmas afternoon. She reached for Daddy's hand, the ache in her palms somehow familiar.

REMEMBERING

Metal against metal
Loud as blood,
Then, silence,
Quiet—
Autumn leaf falling.
My tricycle, Rocket
Died
On Christmas Day.

Paula Watkins Alfred's most recent publication is her novella "The Raucous Bird and A Felony Tryst" in the mystery/romance anthology *Foxy Statehood Hens and Murder Most Fowl*. She's a coauthor of Chik~Lit for Foxy Hens, a romance anthology. Paula, a longtime Tulsa resident, often incorporates her experience as a veteran criminal defense attorney in her writing and public speaking. Her website is Paulaalfred.com and she loves to hear from readers and other writers.

*Back in Lebanon I was interested in American movies, the
Hollywood westerns and musicals...*

Caravan Cattle Company Under Observation
by Najwa Raouda

Our church singles class had agreed to meet at the Caravan
in Tulsa for a social event. As a newcomer to Tulsa and to
American ways, I asked, "What is Caravan, and where?"

"A dance hall," they said.

Aha, I thought. I like dancing. This should be fun.

So, I arrived at the appointed place and hour, but no one
from the class was in sight. What I saw was a large sign,
"Caravan Cattle Company." In my native Lebanon, a lady does
not dance with or among cattle. But, "When in Rome..."

The Caravan is a building without windows—no way to see
or guess what happens inside except by entering. I began my
observation of this unique American experience after stepping
tentatively through the door.

My first surprise—no cattle. My second surprise was that,
despite hundreds of people inside drinking, the place was
spotless. I quickly learned why when I encountered six large
security men, who have the additional duty of cleaning up any
messes as quickly as possible.

Further inside I found tables of two sizes—intimate four-
person tables, where people sat close and whispered into one
another's ear, and a larger size that accommodated six or more.
All were raised above the customary height with patrons seated
on bar stools. Lighting was adequate in the "socializing" area,
dimmer in the back, and brighter in the inner game room. The
lighting on the dance floor was quite colorful.

As I went into the dancing arena, I discovered a teaching
session led by a nice-looking guy. He stood in the middle of ten
couples and was using a small microphone on his shirt to give
instructions to the group. He was called Cowboy Bob, and I was
told that he always wears a black cowboy hat. Bob walked to
each couple and showed the man how to get his partner under
and around his arm. Everyone could hear Bob's "slow-slow-
quick-quick" instructions for the Two-Step western dance. The

84

music started and everyone got busy, as did Bob, monitoring and correcting each couple's movements. Cowboy Bob took his lessons seriously, teaching with his heart.

Sitting at a small round table, I ordered water with lemon just to have a glass in hand. Although it was early, I realized my church friends were not coming. By now I was so absorbed in the goings-on in this "cattle company" that I decided to stay, observe, and even take notes. On my left sat a woman in jeans trying to say a polite "No" to a man in jeans and a white cowboy hat. He insisted that she could do it, and she was apologetically saying, "It's hard and I couldn't follow the music and the count."

"But let's try," suggested the cowboy.

"Oh, I don't think so."

Another woman with a wide smile approached the couple and commented on the men in the Caravan, "You may not choose them, but you need to deal with them." All three laughed.

From the dance floor, I could still hear continuous instructions. "Turn your lady around, keep her under control, then move her to the left while your hand's in the back," Cowboy Bob demonstrated. I saw the four hands of the couple, and Bob's hands high up trying to let the women pass under and around the men's stretched hands. At that moment I realized dancing was not always fun to teach. One man volunteered to show the couple how to work on the steps by first demonstrating with his partner and then with the lady partner of the new dancers. A couple at the farthest end missed a turn, and I saw the woman start to fall.

"As you are turning around, try not to choke your partner," Cowboy Bob said, with a great sense of concern.

The front doors opened, and two men stepped inside wearing identical white cowboy hats. Both were in their mid-twenties, and their jeans, boots, and attitude reflected the West as evoked by Hollywood. They were talking and heading to an open place right next to the dance floor. They both had beers, and one was smoking. They put down their drinks and cigarettes, looked around as if scanning the place, then rested their hands on their waists and kept on talking. These men seemed the type to take their time to study the place, the faces, and the possibilities before deciding what to do next.

Four girls in jeans and tight shirts occupied the table to my right, gossiping together. They whispered and laughed out loud, but when men looked at their table, they were not interested—there was much more fun in their gossip than dancing or men. After a few minutes, a man approached, and all the girls refused his offer to dance. He backed away, with his hands thrown wide, and laughed. The girls smiled and shouted to him, "Nothing personal," perhaps healing the wound they had not meant to inflict. Later, when one of them left the table to dance, everyone sat ready to do what people are supposed to do at the Caravan—dance and drink.

A woman in her late forties came in and headed toward a high stool right at the counter. She wore heavy makeup and wandered around, looking as if trying to grasp something. Anything. She kept on smiling, inviting to others, but when she did not receive quick responses, she turned her back to the tables and watched the dancing. From time to time, she would look at the entrance as if in anticipation of newcomers and new possibilities. She lit a cigarette, put it out moments later, and turned around. Looking serious, she stood up, indicating her availability. A guy from some distance pointed her way, checking for her approval. She smiled, he approached, and she met him halfway to the dance floor. They danced the shuffle and seemed to enjoy it.

A group of five occupied the big table in the front. They seemed to be very comfortable and to know the place like their own homes. Three women and two men started the group at the table, and soon more individuals dropped by to say hi and to share. A couple started to dance. They were highly skilled and started with the swing. Although the man was in his late fifties, his steps and movements were subtle and very impressive. The woman was much younger, and she was happy to dance to her partner's lead, a professional as I could tell. Other couples from the clique joined in dancing and the spectators watched the soft but sophisticated moves.

Later in the night, I noticed a man busy helping his partner put on her shoes. It turned out she carried a special pair of dancing shoes, and she couldn't put them on because of the dim lights. The situation was funny as they both seemed eager to dance, but the stubborn shoes were still not on. One man wished to attract the attention of a woman who passed by without noticing him, so he dipped a paper napkin in water and threw it on her. She reacted pleasantly. Still, the most significant incident was a man in a wheelchair confidently dancing the Two-Step. His female partner danced to the rhythm, and he didn't miss a turn. Apparently, at a "cattle company" dancing is not only for the blatantly fittest.

Bill, a dance instructor I had met previously, came from the back and hugged me. He asked for a dance, and I accepted. Now I was a participant as well as an observer. The lady sitting to my right had not been comfortable seeing me take notes in the dark. When she asked me what I was doing, I said I was jotting down a few ideas. She didn't seem to trust me, but did not ask further.

Dancing the Two-Step with Bill made me feel as if I had two left feet; dancing Cowboy Cha-Cha left me swinging from one side to the other incessantly. Later, I learned that Bill was also a buffalo breeder, and *that* said it all.

By the end of the evening, a man in his fifties approached me and asked, "Dancing or studying?"

"A little of both," I answered.

He said he understood since he had been a night student and usually carried his books wherever he was; after all he said, "There is not enough time for everything."

I decided to visit the Caravan more often in order to keep up my observations. After three successive nights, I could categorize those who attended as follows:

Floaters: Mostly men, floaters do not sit at a table but wander the room looking for a dance partner for a three-minute-dance. The floaters usually carry a drink along, a beer or coffee, and are in search mode.

People with special partners: These only dance with their girlfriends or escorts. They may dance once or twice as a courtesy with other people they know.

Dance Clique: These groups come together or meet at the Caravan. They sit at the same table, share the same interest in dancing, and respond to movements they know. They work on their dancing outside the Caravan, like in a workshop or other dance centers, and meet at the Caravan for practice. These people, directly or indirectly, entice spectators to join in wherever they practice.

Small Clique: Groups of four to six, these people share the same table and include at least a man or two. The men looked to be the patriarchs of the clique, and the women who stand or sit at their table are invited to dance. These men look for "floater" women, and when they cannot find a partner, they return to their "base." The men go to the Caravan early to secure a table and set up the drinks. They also accompany the women to their cars when as they leave—a nice touch of chivalry.

The Young Group: These men, usually in their twenties to thirties, are less into dancing and more into romancing. They usually stay together with young men their age. They reveal much insecurity in the way they approach women, and they usually gather in a large group to drink, watch, and hang out.

The Drinkers: The drinkers sit by themselves at or close to the bar and are only interested in drinking and talking. They may be looking for romance, but drinking is their primary objective, the sparkling glass their expanding microcosm. They rarely dance, or even watch, but may play pool and drink, bravely interacting with the merry macrocosm around them.

To these groups we must add three that are women-only:

Queens at Court: These women are selective, choosy, emancipated, and empowered from eyelash to heel, though not that the others are not. The queens avoid eye contact with anyone who does not appeal to them. They are usually satisfied with two or three dances for an evening.

The Girls' Network: These young women enjoy one another's company and usually laugh loudly or gossip with heartfelt gestures. As long as they are talking, they usually reject an outsider who tries to approach for a dance. Hence, their penalty for anyone who interrupts the net is banishment and rejection.

Women Who Belong to Dancing or Small Cliques: These women are there to have fun, dance, belong, and socialize. They are always dancing with other members of the clique, and are much fun to watch. These cliques are almost perfect in their dancing ability, and they watch and follow all the steps. Age and looks are not criteria in such groups, but dancing and social skills are.

Still, the most intriguing observation was for body language as the means of communication. People at the Caravan, probably due to loud music, use body language and gestures constantly. It's nice to be at a place where not much language is needed, where issues are not debated, but requests are offered and only an acceptance or a rejection is expected. I wish that real life were like life in the Caravan, where eye contact is anticipated, a slight touch on the shoulder down to the elbow is approved, and a tap on the shoulder is an invitation for a dance. Entering someone's territory is another form of wanting to dance.

One may conclude that the Caravan is where cowboys meet cowgirls. My observation shows that it is also a place for dancing competition and dancing advertising. It is a place to escape boredom and loneliness, and a place where one's name and profession are of the least importance. I observed various emotional objectives: some troll for romance, others to hang out, many to make new friends, and most to practice the art of dancing. Dancing is a fun aerobic exercise with low impact. So why not? I also sensed heightened emotions in whatever the participants were doing, they reflected conflict, jealousy, competition, rivalry, belonging, and tension. The actions ranged from a handshake to a full body press and everything in between. My observations detected changes in moods and emotions, from being rejected one minute, to being uplifted when a woman approached and asked for a dance. Good dancers are envied, and the place reflects the distinct advantage for a man who is a good dancer.

After several visits to the Caravan, I concluded it was a place that transported me from my routine life and responsibilities to a dreamlike spot where one dances, drinks, and has a good time without having to think or do much. Although at first I was upset with my church friends for failing to show up where we had decided to meet, I was thankful I got to experience life in the Caravan. I first felt I was the fool who "rushed in where angels fear to tread," but later I realized my adventure was an opportunity of an exciting experience that educated me more about life in Tulsa, Oklahoma. Back in Lebanon I was interested in American movies, the Hollywood westerns and musicals, but all those timeless classics would not have enriched me as much, nor touched me as closely. Now, my experience affirms that I, as an immigrant, have crossed the river to the West, where life can never be as predictable as it used to be for an exceptionally conservative, single-mother from the Land of Cedars.

Najwa Raouda was born in Lebanon and is now a U.S. citizen. She received her PhD from Oklahoma State University. Dr. Raouda is an international consultant on the Middle East, oil, comparative literature, and world religions (Islam in particular). Among other courses, she teaches Arabic Language and Culture at OSU.

"I've been told I should take photographs or write a book about creating them—do something besides build one, tear it down, and build another."

The Two-Sided Jigsaw Puzzle
by Romney Nesbitt

We met in the Border's café on 21st Street in Tulsa and settled into two comfy leather chairs in the corner. Many years had passed since Jennie and I had worked together. As a result of reading an article I had written on the challenges of living the creative life, Jennie requested an hour of creativity coaching.

"Are you still painting?" she asked.

"Yes, watercolors—mostly portraits and I'm doing more writing these days."

"Are you working?"

I told her I taught art to fifth and sixth graders and was building my coaching practice. Her question was an important one. She was making sure I had found a way to juggle a job and my creative pursuits. Nestled back in the big leather chair warming both hands with her coffee, she seemed satisfied with my answer and ready to move on.

"What would you like to talk about?" I asked.

She sat up and scooted to the edge of the chair, planted her feet, and looked around. The café wasn't very crowded. The semi-private space we had claimed was still ours. "I took up painting watercolors a few years ago." She told me her part-time job was to manage her husband's landscape design practice. She answered the phone, made appointments, greeted people, took care of the e-mail messages, and kept the waiting room straightened. "The kids are grown, and I have more time to call my own than I've ever had before—but I'm still not getting any art work done."

"Do you feel cramped by the time you spend at your husband's office?"

"No, not really. It helps us financially that he doesn't have to hire anybody to do the little stuff. It's fine. I probably just need to use my time in the evenings better."

"Most of us could do a better job of managing our free time."

"I especially enjoy one part of what I do at the office."

My interest perked. "What part is that?"

"While I'm at the office, I make little 'centerpieces' for the waiting area."

"Centerpieces?"

"Yeah, there's a square table in front of the couch. I covered it with a cloth, and make arrangements of sea shells or seeds—natural stuff with a candle in the middle.

"Sounds beautiful."

"Some people don't realize it's special. They put their drinks on the cloth! So I made a big production out of putting coasters on the end tables to keep their cans off my centerpiece."

"How often do you make these centerpieces?"

"Not often enough for some people." She laughed. "Some of the regulars expect a new one every time they come in!"

"So, you do a couple a month?"

She nodded. "I've been told I should take photographs or write a book about creating them—do something besides build one, tear it down, and build another."

"Are you interesting in writing?" She shook her head. "Want to take photographs?" Another shake. "Then, tell me, what do you think your centerpieces do for people?"

"The centerpiece is a visual resting space, a place to be still and get away from the rush of life. My little arrangements are an invitation to relax, look at something beautiful, and leave the cares of the world behind."

"By building these, it sounds like you're making a real contribution to the work your husband does. You set the stage for what happens next. The centerpiece holds the space."

"Holds the space?"

"That's a spiritual direction term. My spiritual director always had a little arrangement of cloth and a cross and candle in her office when I would go in for my appointment. She said it held the space for the Divine."

She thought about this for a minute. "I can see that."

The late afternoon crowd was coming in the café. An older lady with her arms full of books and an extra large coffee sat down in one of the nearby chairs leaving only one unoccupied chair as a buffer zone, too close now for the direction the conversation was going. I said, "Let's walk and talk."

We picked up our purses and coffees and left the area. We walked past the elevator to the winding staircase and went up. The upstairs at Border's has a different feel. It's a quieter area, full of books on world religion and metaphysics as well as CDs. The chairs on this level are Shaker style, serviceable and serious. We chose two that overlooked the stairwell, by a sale display.

I changed the subject. "Tell me how long it takes you to do the office chores each day."

She did some mental calculation. "A couple of hours, off and on, in between appointments."

"And you're there for how long every day?"

"Four or five hours."

"Once you get people settled and they go into the office, how much time do you have?"

"Forty minutes or so."

"What do you do then?"

"I read. Some days I make the centerpieces, but that's only every once in a while. My daughter told me to take my drawing table to the office."

Bingo. "Sounds like you've got some time on your hands to do some art if you want, in between your work."

"But I don't know what to paint."

This is the moment I live for. *She doesn't know what to paint?* I paused as I thought of the best way to phrase the obvious.

"The way you described your centerpiece reminds me of a still life."

She threw her hands up in the air as if she had walked into a hold-up, "Oh, I don't draw well enough to do a still life. All that perspective! I couldn't possibly paint one of my centerpieces."

The art teacher inside me kicked in. "You could simplify the composition by drawing a bird's-eye view of the still life, looking down. No perspective problems." Her eyebrows went up in a hopeful slant. I continued, "Something small, maybe 12 x 12? Doable in short amounts of time?" I made this suggestion with a slight lift at the end of my sentence. I was trying to create an opening for her to walk through. This had all the makings of a "both/and" moment.

"That does sound easier." She nodded her head, ever so slightly, then looked up and to the right, at something invisible to me. I hoped she was visualizing herself at her drawing table in the office waiting room, happily painting the still life she had created both for the benefit of her husband's clients and for herself.

Have you ever worked one of those two-sided jigsaw puzzles? The puzzle has pictures on the front and back sides— imagine a New England fall landscape on one side and a man in a hot air balloon on the other. When all the pieces from one side are in place, side two is also finished.

Jennie had been working on a puzzle of a scene of the "productive" life she lived while she worked at her husband's office. At the same time her mind was secretly putting together a very different puzzle of a new creative life. With each "centerpiece" she created, she was making mental preparations to draw and paint. Arranging and rearranging the objects on the cloth gave her an opportunity to practice her compositional skills. The appreciation from visitors to the office built her self-confidence as an artist.

Like a puzzle with two sides, our everyday lives and our creative lives exist simultaneously. Once we're able to see all the hours of our day as one continuous stream of mini-opportunities for creativity and productivity, our day jobs can no longer keep us separate from our creative inner lives. Jennie realized she had time and space for both. Living life in the flow of creativity, our efforts and ideas work together creating a two-sided puzzle.

Romney Oualline Nesbitt is a minister, art teacher, and creativity coach. In her coaching practice, she helps writers and artists move past perceived limitations to reach their creative goals. Nesbitt writes a coaching column for *Art Focus Oklahoma* and teaches courses on creativity for Tulsa Community College. Her book, *Conquer the Challenges of the Creative Life: Tips from a Creativity Coach*, will be published in 2008 by AWOC.COM.

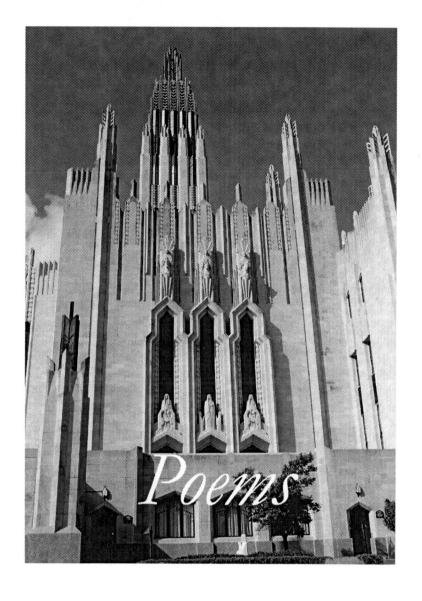

Poems

169 Highway Kansas City to Tulsa
by Sally Jadlow

Two ranchers amble through
a dew-filled pasture
on quarter horses.

A thousand hand mirrors
dance in morning sun
on a farm pond.

Birds swoop in tandem
to an unseen choreographer
through fall breeze.

Six rotund hay bales
on a narrow trailer
like a hairy behemoth
on its way to hungry cattle.

Fleecy clouds play hide and seek
with afternoon sunshine
as far as Nowata.

Rusty oil wells
suck black syrup from the earth.

At Oologah-Talala high school
reduce speed
to twenty-five miles an hour.

Three jet contrails streak
the pale blue sky.

Four-lane highway ribbons
over long rolling hills
toward horizon.

Around a curve,
over a rise,
shades of Tulsa
jut from the landscape.

Sally Jadlow is the award-winning author of *The Late Sooner* and *Sonflower Seeds*, plus many published poems, short stories, and devotionals. She teaches creative writing to both adults and children and serves the Kansas City area as a chaplain to corporations. Sally's website is SallyJadlow.com.

The Secret You Auto Know
by Beverly Strader

Cars have driven Tulsey Town
for about a hundred years.
Model T's to SUV's,
our century, shifting gears.

Horseless carriages on Main
amused the first oil barons.
Baby Boomers in muscle cars
ruled Brookside's Restless Ribbon.

From teenagers at the mall
to bootleggers at their trade,
Tulsa drivers have always known…
Best place to park? In the shade.

Beverly Strader is an "Okie from Kentucky" who works by day at FlightSafety. She's been writing since childhood. At age four, she had a book in her hometown library, which she wrote, illustrated, and published. The librarians made a place for it on a lower shelf and let her "check it out" whenever she pleased. Beverly and her family live on the edge of downtown Tulsa and share the house with their cat, Chip aka His Royal Wideness.

Tulsa's Heartbeat
by Carol Lavelle Snow

The music of Tulsa's churches...
And what churches they are.
Boston Avenue Methodist—tall elegant,
Kirk of the Hills--picturesque,
big, auditorium churches like Victory,
small buildings with steeples,
churches in shopping centers,
churches in schools.

You hear organs and violins,
drums and guitars,
Mendelssohn and Gaither.
Everywhere voices, instruments
lifted in adoration and praise.

Songs spill out into the malls
and offices on Monday morning,
where people in restaurants talk Bible
and bless their food before they eat.

Oh, yes, Tulsa has oil in her veins,
but the pulse of the city is her churches.

With a BFA & MFA in drama from the University of Oklahoma, Carol Lavelle Snow has extensive and varied acting experience and has played Aunt Eller in Discoveryland's *Oklahoma!* for eight years. She also writes and directs shows at the Spotlight Theatre. She has published several short stories and one book, *The Search for Hezekiah's Gold*. Her poems have won numerous awards including a first place at OWFI (2007) and the Helen Downing Award (2007).

Tales

Hector stood. Moses in a rowboat. *If he didn't do something, blood was going to be shed, and he didn't want it to be his.*

Happily Never After
by Carol Johnson

Judge Hector Clintworth looked from Bobby Hemphill to Bobby's soon-to-be-ex-wife, Wylodean, then back to Bobby. "In forty-two years on the bench in Tulsa County, I've never had the misfortune to be shut up in a room with anybody as bent on driving me crazy as you two." *Divorce dot com, my ass.* "You should've had this all settled before you filed the papers." He ticked the items off on his fingers. "Property. Custody. Support. Should have been resolved." He glared at them and continued. "But here you sit. So what we're going to do is, we're going hash this out like rational human beings. You got it?"

Bobby inspected his Tony Lama boots then focused a little to one side of Hector, narrow, dark face bunched up like a peach pit. "Tell Wylodean. She ain't give me a peaceful minute in fifteen years." He cast a malevolent gaze at the blonde in the chair next to his.

"Make him quit callin' me 'Wylodean,'" she said, folding her arms over tube-top encased, bought-and-paid-for breasts.

Hector averted his eyes. Those things were under more pressure than a bottle of Coca Cola left in the sun in August. Put a man's eye out when they blew, for a fact.

"It's your name," Bobby said, enunciating each word as if she were deaf.

"It ain't done it, you pinhead. I ain't been Wylodean since I got into show business. My name's Starla, and I ain't answerin' to nothin' else." She tossed her shaggy blonde hair and gave Hector a great big "I ain't jailbait, but I ain't bad" smile.

Hector stifled a groan. "Now, look," he began.

Bobby cut him off, casting a belligerent stare at the woman beside him. "Just 'cause you got a star tattooed on your ass and a belt that says 'Starla,' don't make it your name." Bobby rolled his toothpick to the other side of his mouth. "And takin' your clothes off in front of a buncha pipeliners ain't show business, it's—"

"The definition of show business is not at issue here," Hector said. We—"

Wylodean/Starla raised halfway out of her chair, her projectile breasts aimed at Bobby, her leather skirt climbing another inch or two toward indecent exposure. "Why, you needle-nosed dipshit! You think bein' a rodeo clown makes you some kinda authority on the entertainment industry?" The skin from her chest up to her neck and face flushed in a way that alarmed Hector, but his fascination with the disastrous potential had him in a chokehold. "Gettin' chased across an arena full of cow shit by an aggravated bull don't qualify you for diddly!" Her breasts heaved as she faced Bobby and gripped the arms of his chair with scarlet-tipped nails. "It sure don't qualify you for smart, you pencil necked..."

Hector stood. *Moses in a rowboat.* If he didn't do something, blood was going to be shed, and he didn't want it to be his. He lifted a huge volume of Oklahoma statutes from a bookshelf and slammed it onto his walnut desk. Sudden silence followed the echoing thud. Both heads jerked in his direction and, tentative control regained, he slid the book to the far side of his desk. "Now look here. We're fixing to have us a civilized conversation, and if we don't, neither one of you will walk out of this place with Molly. You got that?" He glared at them until he had forced a reluctant nod from each, and then leaned back. He pointed at Bobby. "You first."

Wylodean opened her mouth, seemed to reconsider, and closed it. Bobby took a deep breath. "Judge, I spent more money on Wonder Bras and peroxide than Wylodean..." he gave her a look that had probably stopped many a pissed-off bull in its tracks "...will make as long as she lasts in that 'gentleman's' club, as she calls it, and all I want is Molly. I love her, and Wylodean knows it, and that's the only reason she wants her."

Wylodean closed her eyes briefly, as if gathering her great store of wits and patience, then opened them and spoke through barely parted lips. "I am on my way to the top, and you know it. My manager says..."

"Leroy McNabb couldn't manage a belch if he drank a case of Budweiser," Bobby told her. "And the only way you're ever gonna get to the top of anything is if that nitwit rolls over on his

back." Bobby turned imploring eyes on Hector. "Look, Judge."
He began ticking items off finger by finger. "I give her the place
up at Eufaula. She's still livin' in the house out in Bixby. She's
got the Jet Ski, the pontoon, everything. All I want is Molly."

"I worked for all that stuff same as you did, and I didn't take
a single thing I wasn't entitled to." She crossed one long leg over
the other and tossed her hair again. "I have followed you from
Tulsa to Tucumcari to Calgary, pulling that damned trailer till I
was ready to fall over." She sniffed. "I earned everything I got.
You didn't give me nothin'."

The muscles in Hector's neck were tighter than a duck's
butt, and he twisted his neck from one side to another, hoping to
loosen them. "Now listen," he began.

"How about my arc welder?" Bobby asked. "Huh? And my
collection of Louis L'Amour books? Answer me that!" He ran a
hand through his hair and spoke to Hector. "I had ever' book that
man ever wrote, Judge, ever' single one of 'em. She took 'em,
and my arc welder, and a Blue Tick hound she didn't have no
business..."

"Them books were gifts from me to him, and my daddy left
that arc welder to *me*. I give it to Bobby out of the goodness of
my heart."

"Damned Indian giver," Bobby muttered.

"Plus, he traded my weddin' rings for that goddamned
dog..."

Bobby sprang from his chair, fists clenched. "You threw 'em
in the garbage disposal!"

"All right! Stop it. The both of you. Just stop it." Hector
inhaled deeply and closed his eyes. This was going to be like
talking a dog off a meat wagon, damned if it wasn't. Exhaling,
he looked at the pair. "This has nothing to do with an arc welder,
or a dog, or a bunch of books. We're trying to decide on the fate
of an innocent..."

"But, Judge, a woman that'd sell a man's dog at a yard sale
will do most anything. Molly ain't safe..."

"Ain't safe?" Wylodean shrieked. "Ain't safe? You think
she'd be safe with a pencil-neck pinhead like you? You wanna
tell the judge here about the time you got drunk and lost her in
Oklahoma City?" Wylodean's breasts moved under the tube top

like cantaloupes in a tow sack, and in spite of himself, Hector found his gaze glued to the taut red material. So what if she wasn't born with them? They were, in fact, magnificent.

"Judge? Are you listenin' to me?" Bobby asked.

"Of course I am," Hector said. Wylodean smirked, an action that just irritated the hell out of Hector. He stood. "We are done with this conversation. Get out of here so I can think." Stubbing out one cigarette he tapped another from the pack and lit it. "I'm going to sit here, and I'm going to consider all the facts in this case, and then I'm going to render a decision." Both Wylodean and Bobby started to speak, but Hector held a hand up, palm toward the pair. "Ah, ah," he said. "I don't want to hear it." He looked at each of them in turn. "You be back here in an hour. And don't by God be late." He hoped he looked as mean as he felt. "You got that?"

"But Judge, you ain't..." both began, running a verbal footrace to see who could voice the first objection to being so unfairly treated.

God, they gave him a pain in the ass. "Out," he said through clenched teeth. "Get out of my chambers and don't come back for an hour. No more, no less." He glared until the couple had stomped out, then tilted his chair back and drew a deep breath. "God bless a milk cow," he said aloud. "Will I ever make retirement?" Bringing the chair forward, Hector fiddled with the ceramic ashtray in front of him, a replica of the state of Oklahoma, and considered his own question. Oh, hell yeah, he'd make it, if only to spite that dipshit of a district attorney downstairs. He shoved the ashtray away and wished once more that he'd never quit smoking.

He rose and stretched, then went to the window, gazing out at the street below. The door opened and closed softly behind him, and he felt, rather than heard, Pete, his bailiff, approach and stop at his shoulder.

"Jesus, Hector, them two are about a pickle shy of a picnic, ain't they?"

Hector sighed. "They are that. And I'll give you dollars to doughnuts they spend the next forty years side by side, making each other miserable."

Pete sighed. "Well, at least somebody'll be happy."

"Even if it is just the goddamn monkey." Hector shook his head and watched Wylodean and Bobby cross the parking lot below, Molly swinging between them, her simian face the picture of glee.

Carol Johnson is the author of *Everlasting*, a novel released in 2006 and a finalist for the Oklahoma Book Award; a nonfiction book, *Autism: From Tragedy to Triumph*, released in 1994; and numerous articles and short stories. She teaches writing and creative writing at Tulsa Community College and has been a member of Tulsa NightWriters since 1990.

"We can work with him, but most likely, it can't be fixed. It's in his blood."

A Free Horse
by Michele J. Rader

"Kinda skinny, isn't he?" Amber asked.

She ran her fingers lightly over protruding ribs that resembled a picket fence, then drew her hand back and shivered. Nearly fifteen, she knew many of the horrors this world held, but still could not comprehend it all. She wondered how anyone could be so cruel to an animal.

"Well, yes," her mother said, handing her the lead rope. "He's a rescue horse. Aunt Sherri told the women over in South Tulsa to surrender him or she'd call the sheriff. Sherri loaded him up, and the lady said 'good riddance.'"

Amber took the rope. *At least I finally have a horse.* She shook her head and wondered what use a haggard, old horse like this could be. He'd just stand around munching every blade of grass in Oklahoma, that was for sure.

"Look," her mother said, opening the stall door. "I know you had your heart set on Mr. Freeman's little filly, but by the time he has Nellie Rose ready to ride this fall she'll be way out of our price range."

"You're right," Amber admitted. "Guess that explains this free horse."

Her mother *had* kept her promise of getting Amber a horse for her fifteenth birthday. But she had dreamed about owning Nellie Rose since the day the foal was born. The filly gleamed copper, with four white socks and a white star right in the middle of her forehead. To Amber, Nellie Rose was ultimate equine perfection.

Looking at the sorry plug at the end of her rope, she led the emaciated animal into the stall, rubbed his bony withers and sighed. She'd always wanted a horse of her own, but when this one arrived, she'd felt no joy. It wasn't Nellie Rose.

"I nicknamed him Cougar Boy." Her mom spread some fresh shaving in his stall.

Amber eyed his matted coat and wondered if he'd ever been brushed. Dried clumps of mud dotted Cougar's chestnut face, his head seemingly too large for the shrunken body.

But then she looked into his eyes. Deep pools of soft brown reflected his worry and sadness. She tried to turn away but couldn't.

Her heart seemed to melt around the edges, and she knew this little gelding needed her as much as she needed him. Her soul wept for the neglect he'd suffered, the injustice he'd endured.

Cougar brushed his muzzle over her arm and nickered softly, as if thanking her for caring. Amber's eyes brimmed with tears as she lightly rubbed his ears. "It's okay now Cougar Boy. You're going to be just fine." Silently she vowed to nurse him back to health.

For starters, she loaded six cleats of hay in his feeder and dumped a half-pound of sweet feed in the bucket. After supper, she'd slip him a few slices of apple or some crisp carrots. She smiled inwardly knowing Cougar would be thrilled with the treats.

"He must think he's died and gone to heaven." Her mom crossed arms over her chest. "I sure hope we know what we're doing."

Amber set a daily routine of food, water, and gentle petting, as she and her new horse got to know each other. Cougar Boy began to nicker a welcome each time she came to see him. After one short week, his sharp bony edges didn't seem quite as jagged. He still gulped his food, so she dropped a couple fist-sized rocks in the bottom of his feed bucket to slow him down a bit and prevent him from choking.

The medicated baths healed his flaking skin, and a soft brush on his cheek healed his broken spirit. Wrapping her arms around Cougar's neck, the hug seemed to comfort them both. Seeing him put on weight was like watching a miracle take place. His nervousness decreased, and he began to relax when his belly was full.

Later that week they had the vet out. Cougar was vaccinated, de-wormed, and his hooves were trimmed.

"This horse would have died if your aunt hadn't found him when she did," Dr. Sauer commented. "He's just a young fellow, too. By the looks of his teeth, I'd say he's only three."

"Three?" Amber exclaimed. "He looks ancient."

The vet nodded. "Just keep giving him all the hay he wants and gradually bump up his grain intake. He'll be a new horse in no time at all." Dr. Sauer transferred the tattooed markings inside Cougar's upper lip onto the chart. "This gelding here has an ID number from when he was registered. You got yourself a purebred Thoroughbred, Amber."

A Thoroughbred! A real race horse! She envisioned herself perched high on his back, hooves pounding up a cloud of dust as they crossed the finish line.

She glanced at Cougar wondering how fast he might be able to run once he regained his strength. He had his head down to eat, munching away, his eyes half closed.

"Momma, can horses smile?" Amber asked. "I swear Cougar Boy's grinning."

"Absolutely, her mom replied. "That's because he has himself a real home now."

Spring in Oklahoma brought on lush green grass and yellow sunflowers. Every day Amber tended Cougar, feeding, brushing, loving him, and every day he seemed to enjoy her company. The pair spent quiet hours all summer under the shade of tall ash trees; Amber read a book while Cougar ate voraciously to regain his lost weight.

After four months, he had finally gained enough muscle mass for Amber to attempt to saddle him. He didn't seem to mind the leather on his back or the bit in his mouth.

Her mom helped saddle Cougar and adjusted the headstall.

"Seems to me he's been ridden before," Amber told her. "I just hope he remembers." Gingerly, she climbed on Cougar's back while her mom lengthened the stirrups.

"Go easy now. We don't want any trouble on the first go-round."

Amber strapped on her helmet and nodded. "Walk," she said to Cougar Boy. When nothing happened, she gave a gentle squeeze with her legs.

He leaned back on his hindquarters and threw them both into a whirling frenzy that nearly made her lose her seat. "Whoa, Cougar! Whoa!" He charged on, as if a pack of wolves were snapping at his heels. She shifted her weight, pulled back on the reins, and jammed her heels downward. Cougar ignored the cues and sprinted around another lap. She fought down the panic that rose within her pounding chest. She grabbed the inside rein and swung him in a tight circle. The horse finally stopped.

"Guess he forgot how to 'whoa'," her mom said. She looked a bit worried and amused at the same time.

Determined to get it right, Amber pointed Cougar the opposite way and gave another gentle squeeze but again he reacted as if she had given a swift kick in the gut. Off like a shot, he circled the arena like a BB in a boxcar. "Whoa, boy! Easy!" Cranking the right rein to the center, they skidded to a halt.

"Maybe he's not ready yet," she said, reading the disappointment on her mother's face.

"I'm afraid he is," Mom replied. "My guess is he's been trained to race. It's a conditioned response for race horses." She frowned, trying to explain. "Each time he was ridden, they'd spur or whip him to run. That's why he breaks into a tear. We can work with him, but most likely, it can't be fixed. It's in his blood."

They had come so far; it didn't seem fair. Amber dismounted and ran her fingers down Cougar Boy's sleek neck. She unfastened the girth and removed the saddle. Her hopes of ever riding him dissolved as she watched him graze. Maybe, just maybe, he'd change. But in her heart she knew it wasn't likely.

Inside the house, she eyed the health folder that contained Cougar's medical records. Opening it to the first page, she wondered about the strange tattooed numbers that Dr. Sauer had transcribed from Cougar's lip months ago. If she could look them up on the Internet, she'd find out what Cougar's real name was, and maybe where he'd been born.

She signed onto the computer and typed in *thoroughbreds*. Following a link to *pedigree* led her to PEDIGREE - SEARCH BOOKS, and she typed in the numbers. Nothing.

Next she Googled *horse tattoos*. That brought up a page titled Missing Horses. Curious, she selected it, scrolled down the numerous listings of stolen and missing horses, and clicked on the Oklahoma link. Pages of equines stared back at her like the children's faces on the back of milk cartons.

"What are you looking up?" Her mom came in and sat beside her.

"I can't believe how many people are looking for stolen horses. I thought that only happened back in the Wild West."

Mom shook her head. "Unfortunately it still happens."

Amber scrolled down and froze. "This horse looks just like Cougar. He has the same markings and white snip on his muzzle." The tattoo markings, A50536 matched.

Her mom reached over and took control of the mouse. "It *is* Cougar! Only his real name is Ace. Someone stole him from the rack track." She verified his birth date, and frowned. "That would make him just about three and a half years old now."

The article read: *Ace was stolen from Will Rogers Downs in Claremore, OK on May 18, 2005. Owner is heartbroken over his loss. Please call if you have seen him. Sarah Hill (918) 555-3478. REWARD!!!*

Her mom scribbled the contact information onto a scratch pad and inhaled deeply. "You know what we have to do, don't you?"

Amber nodded, as tears threatened to spill. *Why did doing the right thing feel so wrong?*

As her mom dialed the phone, Amber stared at the pictures posted on the Internet. Cougar, no, Ace's owner clearly loved this horse and even offered a hefty reward for his return. Her mother was right. Ace needed to go home.

The next day, a silver, three-horse trailer backed into the yard. A tall woman in a ball cap hopped out of the driver's seat.

"I didn't want to get my hopes up in case it isn't Ace after all, but tattoos don't lie," Sarah Hill said, trying to stave off her excitement.

Amber and her mom led Sarah to the barn to reclaim her stolen horse.

"Ace! It's really you!" She ran to the horse and hugged him around his neck.

Surprised, Ace let out a loud whinny when he recognized his friend.

"Well, he's never forgotten you," her mom said, then glanced at her daughter. "And I know Ace will never forget you either, Amber."

It felt like her heart was breaking, and she hoped her mom's words held true.

"I can't thank you enough for all you've done, so please take the reward money," Sarah said pressing a manila envelope, holding twenty-five hundred dollars cash, into Amber's hands.

She looked from the cash to Ace and shook her head. "No." Amber handed back the envelope. "Keep it. We didn't do anything." Knowing his owner was coming, she had already said her goodbyes to Ace.

She gave Sarah a forced smile, hung her head, and walked away.

Sarah and Amber's mom loaded Ace and chatted for a bit. Then the owner drove off with her horse, honking and waving.

Amber plopped into a folding chair by the front porch and sniffled. "That was the best horse I ever had," she said, knowing mascara smudges were ringing her eyes like a raccoon.

"That's because it was the *only* horse you ever had," her mom remarked.

"I know," she said, her voice scratchy. "But I really loved him. He was special." She bent forward and used the hem of her tee shirt to wipe her nose.

"That was kind of you to refuse the reward, you know."

"Yeah, well, I'm guess I'm just a nice person," she said trying to lighten the mood.

"And sometimes nice people should be rewarded," her mother said pulling up a chair beside her daughter under the huge ash trees. They sat shaded in comfortable silence in the hot September afternoon. A few cars passed their place, then a red two-horse trailer leisurely pulled into their circular drive. Mr. Freeman got out and waved.

"Howdy, ladies," he said tipping his hat. "Got word you needed a delivery. Where do you want me to put Nellie Rose?"

Amber jumped up in disbelief. "Nellie Rose? Here?"

"Why, yes," he said, stifling a smile. "Paid for in cash by a Mrs. Sarah Hill. She said it was the very least she could do, you looking after Ace and all."

Amber couldn't believe she'd heard right and ran to the trailer to see for herself. Yes, Nellie Rose was really here! She paused, afraid it was all some sort of a cruel joke.

"You can get her out. She's all yours," Mr. Freeman said. With shocked disbelief, she turned to her mother. Mom nodded.

She wrestled the trailer latch open as fast as her fingers could work it, swung back the bar, and then backed out the pretty paint mare. Amber clung to her neck and sobbed for Ace, who had finally made it home against all odds. She also shed a few grateful tears for the surprising hand fate dealt her.

"Nellie Rose," Amber whispered. "I can't believe you're really mine!" With the lead rope in hand and a skip in her step, Amber headed toward the barn with her free horse.

Michele Rader, a freelance writer and animal lover, grew up near Los Angeles, California. After moving to rural Oklahoma fifteen years ago, country living has made a positive impact on her lifestyle and influenced her writing. Michele and her family reside on a small horse ranch outside of Tulsa.

Dane was reminded of why he hated the place so much. The reek of disinfectant invaded his nose, and old eyes watched him as he walked down the hall.

Old Guys and Dead People
by Donna Welch Jones

"You have to go," Mom said. Her hands were planted on her hips, and her voice low and firm.

Pulling himself to a sitting position on the sofa, Dane's words shot back. "I get one freakin' day off from school because it's Veteran's Day, and you want me to spend it with old guys and dead people!"

"Dane, I'm sure the dead soldiers at the cemetery will remain in the ground. They're going to be honored, not dug up."

"Not funny Mom. You said I could go skateboarding."

"That was before I found out the Navy is honoring your grandpa today. We both need to be there for him." Mom started walking toward the kitchen.

Dane raised his voice, "You know Papa doesn't care if I'm there or not. He doesn't even like me."

She turned with a swirl. "Don't talk like a jerk, Dane. You know he loves you. He even asked me if you're coming to the ceremony. Anyway, I need you to help me get him in and out of the car and onto the stage. He doesn't get around too well at eighty-three."

"You promised I could go skateboarding today!" Dane's lowered his eyelids and thrust out his lips.

"Okay, since I'm breaking a promise, I'll pay you twenty dollars if you'll help."

Dane only hesitated for a moment. Twenty dollars for a couple of hours of boredom was something he could handle just fine.

"I'd like the money in advance."

"Here it is." She handed him a twenty from her wallet.

Two hours later he was dressed in his blue shirt and khakis, and in his Mom's car heading toward the nursing home.

"You should've told me I was going to have to dress up," Dane complained.

114

"If I'd told you. it would've probably cost me more money."

"That's for sure," Dane grumbled.

When they arrived at the nursing home Dane was reminded of why he hated the place so much. The reek of disinfectant invaded his nose, and old eyes watched him as he walked down the hall.

Papa stopped rocking long enough to raise his hand in greeting when his daughter and grandson walked into his room.

"Been chasing any nurses lately?" Dane teased.

"Nah, they're all too fast for me," he said with a toothless grin.

"Where are your dentures?" Mom asked.

"Over there in the cup. I don't like 'em, because they feel like a rock in my mouth. I guess I should wear them today though."

"Dane help Papa with his teeth while I get his house slippers on him."

"I'll help with the shoes not the teeth," Dane said, his mouth puckering in disgust.

The old man's feet were so deformed from arthritis he had to wear dark house shoes instead of regular shoes. Dane tried to push Papa's foot forward in the shoe, then he tried to pull the back around the heel.

"I'm sorry; I'm no help, Dane. My old feet just can't push much anymore." Papa stared at his feet.

"I thought I couldn't get them on because you've got big feet like mine," Dane laughed.

Papa looked at Dane's feet. "You're right my boy! I never realized that my feet are as big as yours. No wonder my shoes don't fit."

Dane finally slid the shoes on his grandpa. Mom helped him put on the jacket of his old dress uniform. The dress hat and pants had disappeared years ago.

"Where's my sailor hat?"

"I don't think you need it today Dad."

"I gotta have my hat," the old man said, his lips set in a determined line.

After much searching, Mom pulled the hat out from under a pile of underwear in the bottom drawer of the chest.

It took both Dane and his mom to maneuver Papa into the wheelchair. Dane pushed it down the hall and into the parking lot. After getting the old man into the car, Dane had to fold the wheelchair and put it in the trunk. Now he was sure he should've held out for more money.

The drive east on 51st Street in Tulsa seemed like a long one to Dane. His grandpa's heavy breathing and Mom playing old people music made for a tedious trip. As they approached Floral Haven Cemetery, the browns of autumn changed to red, white, and blue.

"What's the deal with all the flags?" Dane asked.

"There's one flying for each veteran buried at the cemetery," Mom answered.

The blowing wind caught the hundreds of flags and unfurled them to attention.

"Beautiful," Papa said. "Beautiful."

After Dane unloaded the wheelchair and helped get the old man seated, he pushed the chair toward his Mom. "Your turn to work."

She pushed the wheelchair in the direction of the stage. A short, muscular man in dress uniform approached them.

Papa said, "Stop." He placed each hand on a wheelchair arm and struggled to stand. By the time the officer got to them, the old man was ready to salute.

"It's an honor and a privilege Lieutenant Reynolds to have you with us today," Commander Sparks said.

"The honor is mine sir."

Dane lagged behind as Commander Sparks escorted Papa and Mom to the stage.

"Excuse me," a voice said.

"What?" Dane turned to see a girl of about his age.

"I'm Megan Taylor. I wondered if you would tell Lt. Reynolds 'thank you' for me."

"I guess. Why?"

"He saved my grandfather's life during World War II. If it weren't for him my father, brothers, and I would never have been born. Grandfather told me many times how Lt. Reynolds retrieved a live hand grenade and threw it away from four injured sailors. He also told me that Lt. Reynolds was the bravest man he ever knew."

"Yes, I'll tell him," Dane said. He felt a tightening in his chest. He walked quietly onto the stage and sat down beside his grandpa. He touched Papa's shoulder, and his grandpa reached up and squeezed his hand.

Commander Sparks started the program. "We're here to honor all veterans, but today we give special recognition to a man of untold bravery whose love for his country and care for his fellow sailors make him a super hero among the thousands of veteran heroes. Please stand for an American Super Hero, Lt. Daniel Reynolds."

Dane rose with the hundreds of others who stood and applauded for his grandpa. Papa took Dane's arm as he struggled from the chair and didn't let go as they walked toward the podium. The old man continued to hold onto him while the audience cheered.

Commander Sparks continued, "Through some unfortunate oversight, that was brought to our attention by the families of the four men whose lives you saved during World War II, you never received what you truly deserved. It's my privilege to present you with the Medal of Honor."

"I thank you for this honor. My grandson Dane is here with me today." He turned, no longer facing the audience but looking directly into the boy's eyes. "Today I'm passing on to my grandson the Medal of Honor and my sailor hat, so he will always remember the men, women, and his Papa who fought to keep America free."

Dane pressed an escaped tear into his cheek as his grandpa offered him the medal and hat. "Thank you," he said, then shook his grandpa's outstretched hand.

That afternoon Dane grabbed his skateboard and headed for the door. "I'm off to skateboard."

"Okay," Mom said. "Be home by dinner time."

"No, can do. I'm going to go eat with Papa tonight."

Later, Dane's mom found the note on top of a twenty-dollar bill. It read: Sorry, Your Son, The Former Jerk.

By day, Donna Jones work as a technical supervisor for the Child Development Program with the Oklahoma State Dept. of Health Child Guidance Service. In her free time she is an award-winning writer with numerous stories published in national magazines.

As I watched the wind bend the tops of the trees, I thought how my own life matched the season. But I wasn't ready to stop living.

A Season of Change
by Judy Crews

Why wasn't I happy? I closed my book, laid it on the table, and turned out the lamp. With a sigh, I gazed into the warmth of the fire. I'd been alone most of my life, always waiting for a new knight-in-shining-armor to whisk me off to the adventures that love brings, but it hadn't happened.

Even if my other dreams were unfulfilled, this house had made up for it. Situated in the Cherry Street district of Tulsa, I called it "The Spring House." I'd invested my entire my retirement fund in the venture, and this dream, a successful bed and breakfast including a tea room, had come to pass. Gone were my fears that I would grow old and become terribly boring until both the money and my life were spent.

So why was I restless?

I sang to myself as I worked in the kitchen the next morning. We'd had a few guests throughout the afternoon, but the pace was relaxed. The scattering of tearoom patrons seemed in no hurry to step out into the chilly fall afternoon, especially when they could linger over a pot of tea and melt-in-your-mouth scones.

I prepared for tomorrow's private luncheon when I heard a loud swooshing noise and looked down to find myself standing in a steaming puddle. Water spurted from the hot water heater in the pantry. *So much for my relaxed afternoon.* I slopped my way into the pantry. After a struggle, the valve was turned off, and I stepped back to survey the scene. Well, it could be worse. This could have happened tomorrow with a house full of guests. I splashed to the wall phone and dialed an all-too-familiar number—Jim Williams, all-around handy man and friend.

The neighbor next door had introduced me to Jim. She came to visit soon after I moved in, and found me making a list of repairs and changes needed in the house. I asked if she knew a

119

handyman, and she gave me the name of a retired accountant who had always been a good Mr. Fix-it. He enjoyed doing the things he loved in his retirement years.

In the following months, Jim and I had spent many hours getting acquainted as he repaired, replaced, and renewed the old house. My list dwindled as the house grew more beautiful.

Today, Jim arrived soon after my call and swabbed up the floor while I served my last guests. After clearing the dining area and getting it in order, I returned to the kitchen to see if Jim had found the problem. He had; a faulty soldering job in an elbow joint had given way. In what seemed a very short time, the hot water tank was happy again. We finished mopping up the floor, and I asked if he wanted to stay for a bite to eat.

I always asked, even though he had never accepted an invitation to stay. Nonetheless, he usually agreed to take some goodies "for the road." This time, he hesitated and then agreed. I tried to hide my surprise and realized my smile felt a bit brighter. A blush crept up my cheeks. *Now what was this all about?*

I cut a slice of quiche, put it in the oven to heat along with biscuits from the freezer, and mixed a salad. Jim seemed to enjoy it, and that pleased me more than I wanted to admit. He lingered for a bit and talked. Actually, he seemed reluctant to leave. When he did go, I was left with some strange feelings and wandered over to my best thinking spot.

The floor-to-ceiling windows in the garden tea room were my favorite place to observe the changing weather and sort out problems. In Oklahoma, the one thing we could count on was change. As I watched the wind bend the tree tops, I thought how my own life matched the season, fall, when everything died out. But I wasn't ready to stop living. I felt impatient, ready for a new adventure. I felt changes coming but couldn't be honest with myself and acknowledge what they might be.

The next day I made final preparations for the private lunch and secretly wished I could play hooky. It was one of those wonderful days that made you forget that fall really is the harbinger of winter winds and ice storms in Oklahoma. The sky was a perfect blue and the air so crisp you didn't think about the humidity of the past summer. This year the colors were made-to-order. Every tree glowed in shades of red, gold, and yellow with enough green to say life is not over yet.

The out-of-state group arrived on time. They called themselves *Widows with Wings*, and their presence was a delight. Eleven of them had traveled in a small rented bus—seven women and four men. They were so happy, enjoying each other with a quietness of soul that captivated me. I wondered about the name of their group and how they came to be together. After lunch, they didn't seem in a hurry to leave, so I went to their table and asked if they would tell me their story. Smiles blossomed all around the table; it seemed they could hardly wait to share.

The youngest of the group was a widow in her mid-thirties. When her husband was killed in Iraq, she thought her world had come to an end. She didn't know how she would face the next day. I watched her face, and all I could see, as she spoke, was a soft joy—an expression of deep inner peace. She told of finding comfort in a support group at her church with others who had gone through the death of a spouse. She found healing, but knew she needed more in order to have her heart embrace living.

She wanted to move her focus away from the loss, but wanted the friendship of others who had experienced similar pain. Eventually, she formed a plan she called "Finding Wings Again" based on the feeling that, although her wings had been clipped, they would grow out again. She didn't want to be grounded the rest of her life, rooted to the earth by the pain of lost love.

She had called other widows and widowers and suggested they get together to learn how to live again, not merely survive their losses. They chose to embrace life, God, and others and to live out of their hearts.

Several people at the table told their stories. Each had chosen to reject bitterness and make peace with their pain with the help of God's love. It was the peace that captivated me. It is so rare to find such peace in this world. I was deeply moved by their stories and their willingness to share so openly their journeys of healing and hope. I thanked them for being a part of my day and wished them a wonderful time as they enjoyed the Affair of the Heart craft show.

When they left, I had a stronger sense of the joy of living than I'd felt in a long time. I forced myself to really look at my own heart and my loss. Many years ago, my husband had left me. Although I had healed and moved on in life, I never opened my heart to love again. Oh, there had been some dating, but any time I felt a stirring of emotions, I would break off the relationship. I protected my heart from that sort of suffering at all costs. Now, I realized the price I'd paid.

I wondered if I could ever take that chance again. And, of course, that brought up thoughts of Jim. Reluctantly, I admitted he had been on my mind frequently. I felt more than simple friendship for him. Yet, this time I knew I didn't want to stop the feelings. Just how brave could I be? After listening to the *Widows with Wings*, I decided I simply had to try. I had convinced myself I was at peace, but now I accepted that the only thing that brings true peace is to get beyond the fear of being hurt again.

The Affair of the Heart craft show was at Expo Center was a treat for Jim. Without an invitation, he stopped in to see me after visiting the fair. His eyes were alight with the inspiration of the new woodworking ideas he had seen. He chatted away in the kitchen as I prepped tomorrow's lunch, and he told me all his plans. Cabinets and dollhouses became real as he talked, and renovation ideas emerged for the tree house he had built for his grandchildren. I listened this time, for the first time, with my heart.

A feeling of softness came over me that I cannot explain, but I felt wings begin to grow once again. I was overwhelmed with the revelation that it is never too late to live out of the heart.

What new wonders will tomorrow bring? I can't predict, but I think I'll be in full flight before too long.

Judy Crews is a New England transplant to Tulsa. By day she is a medical billing clerk, but her other life includes writing, being the mother of two daughters, grandmother to one of the world's most beautiful little girls, and volunteering at The Tulsa Healing Center.

I had promised myself on the drive to Tulsa that I was taking a holiday from the blues.

Christmas in July
by Liz Kucera

"You're taking this Christmas in July stuff too far," I laughed as I stood in front of an artificial white tree adorned with red and blue bulbs.

"Maureen, where did you get the cute Uncle Sams dressed like Santa?"

"The Internet, of course," Maureen rolled her eyes. "Sandra, you need to join the twenty-first century. The Internet is the answer for everything these days—shopping, recipes, romance—everything."

"Romance and the Internet?" I wrinkled up my nose. "I hope I'm never that desperate!"

Geri swatted at my arm. "It's quite possible to meet your love match in a chat room."

Oops. Sandra and I exchanged glances. Sounded like that was how Geri had found her most recent husband.

I went back to a safer topic and gestured toward the tree. "It's a little over the top, but the patriotic theme is cute. You're always doing extra for us."

"Glad to have y'all here." She walked over, giving me a little hug. "I'm glad you decided to come. It'll take your mind off *things.*"

Things. Well, that meant my pending divorce. Geri looked expectantly at me, but I had promised myself on the drive to Tulsa that I was taking a holiday from the blues.

Sandra got the hint and changed the subject. "Where's Wyvette? Isn't she joining us?"

"Talked to her this morning. I don't know what's keeping her," Maureen answered.

We sat in the living room reminiscing about old times. We'd grown up together in a little Oklahoma town, Glen's Creek, population about three thousand. Six of us hung together—Maureen, Geri, Sandra, Tammy, Wyvette, and me, Ronnie Mae.

Wyvette was thrust upon us because she was Maureen's cousin and always tagged along.

I'm the only one still living in Glen's Creek, much to my dismay. The husband I found in college decided we should help my parents with the family store. The dreams I had of teaching at a university went by the wayside, and I settled for teaching second grade instead.

The summer of 1980 was a big milestone as we planned our ten-year reunion. But then Tammy was killed in a car wreck, and our reunion was a bleak occasion. Everyone stayed to attend her funeral. Maureen went into a deep depression over Tammy's death, but when she emerged, it was with the decree that we would start our own special celebration. Every July, Maureen was our host.

Now we followed her into the kitchen where the breakfast nook was set with her Christmas china. She'd made a summer style Christmas dinner that included smoked turkey sandwiches, cranberry tea, and pumpkin cheesecake. As we finished lunch, we were discussing whether to go to a movie or relax by the pool when Wyvette finally arrived. She wasn't alone.

There stood Sue Lynn Lamoureaux. I sucked in my breath as if someone had punched me in the stomach. *Sue Lynn Lamoureaux.* In a million years I wouldn't have expected this.

"Season's greetings and surprise!" Wyvette briefly hugged Maureen. "Look who I've brought." I wasn't the only one registering shock.

Wyvette quite smartly avoided my eyes, but Sue Lynn didn't.

"Wyvette," Sue Lynn admonished her. "You told me you'd let Maureen know I was coming."

"But that would have spoiled the surprise."

All heads whipped around to face me. A silence built just like the moments before a tornado dips down from nowhere.

Sue Lynn's contrite expression didn't fool me. I had firsthand experience of the devastation she could wield. She had appeared in Glen's Creek our senior year of high school. While only a sophomore, Sue Lynn had taken one look at my Marty Cafferty and, never mind my plans for the heir to Cafferty Law Firm, went after him like a coyote headed for a hen house. Not that I hadn't put up a fight. I gave up my virginity just to try to hang on to him, but she topped me. Claimed she was pregnant and got him to marry her before his family realized she was lying. Too late. His betrayal stung, and I begged my parents to let me go to college out of state, just so I could get away. I'll never forgive her for that, either.

I'd had plans to go to the University of Tulsa while Marty was in law school, but I couldn't bear the thought of our crossing paths on campus. Their marriage ended, but Marty never came back to Glen's Creek. He couldn't face me, and he couldn't face his father.

The silence was building. I did the only thing I could think to do. I lied.

"I have to go over to Utica Square for a bit. I told Bettye Malicott I'd pick up a package for her at Miss Jackson's before I go back home." I set my jaw in a firm line that dared any of them to call my bluff.

I turned to Sandra and Geri, "Do you want to go with me?"

"Surely you don't have to run right now." Maureen's voice quivered slightly. Her eyes pleaded.

My dearest, and apparently only, friend Sandra, came to my defense. "I'll go. I love Utica Square."

We walked out of the house, and I threw Sandra my keys. I marveled at her composure, but then she didn't have the same history I had with Sue Lynn.

I dug in my purse for shades to protect me from the bright Oklahoma sun, and to hide the tears in my eyes. We sat in silence while I fought to recover.

"Thanks for getting me out of there." As the shock ebbed, I felt angry. I was especially mad at myself for running away, and I cursed Wyvette.

"What possible reason could Wyvette have for bringing Sue Lynn?" I said.

"Beats me. Wyvette has *never* pulled anything like this before. Remember when she told Pamela Burke she was adopted, and Pamela's mom got so mad she cussed out Wyvette and her mom?"

"Yeah, but this is worse."

"Remember when Maureen told her mom she was at Wyvette's house, but she was really with Denny Thomas. Wyvette told, and Maureen almost got grounded from the prom."

"Yeah, but this is worse."

"Remember when she ratted us out to the principal on senior skip day, and we had to spend part of senior week in detention?"

"Yeah, but this is worse."

"Yeah, it probably is." Sandra was quiet and then said, "So what are you going to do?"

I let out a sigh. "I don't know. I don't want to spend one minute with Sue Lynn Lamoureaux—or whatever her name is now. I just wonder about those two."

"Sue Lynn was awful quiet. Maybe she's changed."

"Right, Sandra, maybe she's joined a convent or something."

I moaned and rubbed my temples, experiencing the beginnings of something that had to be a tension headache.

Sandra bit her lip. "What about you and Reed. Are you really splitting?"

"Well, he's moved out. He's selling the store and leaving town in a few months. That's a pretty good clue."

"I'm sorry. I hate to see it happen."

"I need some kind of change. Maybe I'll ask to teach third grade. I've been teaching second since 1974."

Sandra raised an eyebrow, "You need a bigger change than that."

She pulled into the tree-lined drive of Utica Square. We parked and explored the shops.

"It's so pretty here. And at Christmas, it's one of the most beautiful spots in Tulsa."

"Yeah." Memories of shopping here with Mom and Dad flooded over me. There was always something magical about a trip to Utica Square.

"Look." I reached down and picked up a dime. "Dad always said Tulsa was the richest city."

"At the price of gas these days, a dime isn't going to go far."

"It just reminds me of Dad. After his heart attack he took up walking. He collected money he found on the street. Back home he'd find a penny or two, but he found a quarter in Tulsa one time." I smiled to myself. I had lost Dad two years ago and Mom soon after. They'd be so disappointed in Reed now, selling the store and leaving me on my own.

How could I settle all this turmoil in my life? Why had Reed really left? Did he sense something missing in our lives together?

Sandra picked up on my mood. "Think you'll marry again?"

"Where would I meet someone in Glen's Creek? Anyway, I don't relish the idea of starting over. Not at my age. I need quiet time to myself, although being in a small town doesn't offer much privacy."

"Lots of people start over at our age. People get divorced or become widowed. I think you're right, though, to give yourself time to think about it. What about Marty? Think you'll want to look him up?"

"Never!" That was my recurring nightmare. I'd dream we were back together, then he'd go missing, and I'd spend the rest of the dream relentlessly searching for him.

Sandra's cell emitted a chirping sound. "It's Maureen asking if we're coming back soon."

I made a face, rolled my eyes, and said, "Tell her not to worry. We're heading back."

When she relayed the message, I said, "I'm ready to go ask Wyvette just what the hell she was thinking!"

We found them out by the pool. Christmas lights decorated the cabana, but the festive mood had dissipated.

Wyvette ignored my icy glare, and sauntered over. "Before you get all wild-eyed and crazy, there's a good reason I brought Sue Lynn."

"Bringing *her* here is the most despicable thing you've done."

Wyvette gave a deep sigh of annoyance. "If you'll just listen."

"She practically ruined my life—and Marty's."

"Ronnie Mae, that was thirty-seven years ago. Sue Lynn's changed. She's truly sorry. Listen. She'll tell you herself."

"I wouldn't believe a word that came out of her mouth."

Wyvette didn't give up. "You need to unburden yourself. You'll never have peace if you don't. You'll just have one failed relationship after another."

I sucked in my breath at the audacity of her words. "For your information, Sue Lynn *caused* that first failed relationship, and the second one lasted more than thirty years."

"You girls okay?" Maureen interrupted.

I glared at her. "Sure, we're having a great time. Wyvette has decided to make this a Jerry Springer moment for me. She blindsided me, and you're letting her get away with it."

"Ronnie Mae?" It was Sue Lynn.

I steeled myself against her presence. The only way I wanted to see Sue Lynn was tied down on an anthill with me dripping honey across her. The image lifted my spirits. I wheeled to face her.

Maureen dragged away an uncooperative Wyvette.

"I hope some day you can forgive me. I am sorry," Sue Lynn said.

"I won't waste my time forgiving you, but I am a little curious about how you're involved with Wyvette. She can be a bitch at times, but she's not in your league. You've got the makings of an Alexis Carrington!"

She didn't flinch. "It's never a waste to forgive. I can't speak for Wyvette, but we all come to a point when we take stock of where we've been and where we're headed. Recently I've had the chance to examine my life, and know I have wrongs to address. I've learned a little late in life that happiness can't come at the expense of someone else."

"I'm not going to discuss the meaning of life with *you*."

"That was said with a lot of bitterness. I know I did wrong. I was only sixteen years old!"

"Only sixteen, but you changed my life. And Marty's father never forgave him."

"Marty's father didn't understand. Marty didn't want to live his father's dream. He didn't want to take over the law firm."

My mouth dropped open in disbelief. "That's not true. That's all Marty talked about."

"I was Marty's wife. He told me different."

"You were married for what? Three months? Until the annulment? I knew him his whole life." I threw up my hands in a gesture of futility. There was no point trying to discuss anything else with her, and I felt exhausted from the effort.

"Did you tell her yet about talking to Marty?" Wyvette slithered back up to join the conversation. It was more than I could take.

"Maureen! You'd best come get her!" I had a great desire to throw Wyvette in the pool, but it being so hot, she'd probably enjoy that. Left with no other option, I started chasing her around the cabana table.

Maureen and Sandra arrived to form a buffer between us. I think Geri came up just so she could hear better.

Thirty-seven years of hurt bubbled out of me. "Marty? Why would you be talking to Marty? And why would it have anything to do with me?"

Apparently bolstered by the presence of others, Sue Lynn continued, "I located him with the help of the Internet. I wanted to apologize. I found out his wife died, and he's actually living here in Tulsa now."

"I am not interested in Marty!" I said through clenched teeth.

"Well, he's interested in you—after I let him know you were available," Wyvette said.

I felt Sandra give my arm a reassuring squeeze of support, but I felt confused by a buzz of excitement that came from the thought that Marty was close and available. I sat down, and finally sputtered, "How do you know these things? Why are you two in cahoots?"

"Sue Lynn's recovering from breast cancer. I saw her while I was volunteering at the hospital. I told her about our get-togethers. When I found out about you and Reed, I thought you'd be interested."

I didn't know what to say. I weighed the implications. Suddenly it felt like Christmas morning, and I had a stack of presents to unwrap. Maybe there'd be a new life in one of them.

A lump came to my throat. "Okay, I'll think about it. I just don't want anyone trying to force the issue." I glared at Wyvette.

She threw up her hands in surrender, and I gave the best smile I could muster. "I think I've had enough for today. I'm going to head home early."

Maureen was disappointed, but understanding. We said our goodbyes. Sue Lynn slipped me a card with Marty's number. I wished her luck with her recovery. I couldn't see us ever being friends, but breast cancer had taken my mother, so I knew what she was facing.

There was one last present I found on the way to my car. A shiny quarter glimmered in the Tulsa sun. I picked it up and pocketed the coin. *Thanks, Dad. I'll keep it as a reminder that Tulsa is rich with the gifts of friendship and possibilities.*

Liz Kucera grew up in rural Kay County, Oklahoma. She has been an educator in the Tulsa area for more than thirty-four years. Becoming a member of Tulsa Nightwriters has helped her fulfill her dream of becoming a writer. She is cheered on by her mother, husband, daughters and their families, and numerous writing and teaching friends.

The two embraced and a prairie storm of electricity spread through them.

Desire Like the River
by Mark S. Darrah

From deep beneath the highest mountains in Colorado, from the dark, it flows. From the Continental Divide, it rushes rapid and clear down stony peaks and cuts gorges through immortal rock. It rides across the high plains. It subsumes others meandering over the prairie, passing through Dodge City and Wichita. In Oklahoma, it unites with one of a romantic name—the Cimarron—so when it reaches the boundary of the old Muscogee Nation, it is no longer clear and narrow, but wide, silty, and fecund. Waiting for the rains to fill and rush and overwhelm. It may not be the Thames or the Danube. It may not be the Seine, but in Tulsa, on starry summer nights, lovers walk the banks of the Arkansas River as if it might be.

Ryan and Annie did that one Friday night, not all that long ago. On impulse, they had strolled through the fertile, moonlit park which fronted the east bank of that river. He, in an oxford cloth shirt with rolled up sleeves, charcoal slacks, and wing tips. She, in a buttery blouse cut low with frills and lace, a navy skirt, and pumps. Not exactly what either would have selected for a summer's night walk, but exactly what they had chosen for dinner at the most exclusive French restaurant in Tulsa.

The Bistro had been built by new oil money, yet survived the oil patch crashes and booms. Annie had never been there, had never been invited to this pensive, candlelit, and romantic place with fresh cut roses, brittle china, crisp linen, and elegant crystal. Annie had been intrigued. Annie, so sheltered and shy.

Ryan had practiced his French r's so he wouldn't mispronounce the entrees on the menu. Annie had ordered

131

a soda, had not wanted the expensive wine. Had they
known the truth, the waiter's real name was Mel, and on his
days off, he liked to go to the stock car races.

For Ryan, to be seen with Annie and her with him was
ideal delight. The food, perfect. The service, graceful.
Annie, beautiful, sultry, exotic in the dim restaurant. The
candlelight reflected in her eyes like stars in the black
night; flickering shadows teased the fawn colored skin of
her décolletage.

For Annie, the intrigue had not lasted; she hadn't
known what to order. All so formal, so artificial, so stilted.
The food had tasted funny, but she had been charmed
anyway. Even Ryan's voice that evening made her blood
rush. So, when they left, she thought her idea good—a walk
by nature's river, away from the urban artifice, the stilted,
and the artificial.

The Arkansas River sits, ambles, and sometimes roars
by on a treacherous sandy bed two hundred yards wide or
wider. Huge cottonwoods, gnarled hickory trees, and
stubborn oaks, all laced with vines, weeds, and briars, hug
the river. And, on the east bank, just past this wild barrier
of overgrowth, a park lies touching nature and the city.

The air hung heavy and damp as Annie and Ryan
walked the path through the park alongside the river. The
smell of newly mown grass mingled with the teaming,
earthy breath of the underbrush and the fertile waters.

"Do you feel funny down here, all dressed up?" asked
Annie. A cicada shrieked from an anonymous bush.

Ryan shook his head. "Not really. One day, I saw a guy
who looked like a beatnik—bongo drums, dark sunglasses,
beret—walking hand in hand with a woman in a navy
business suit." Ryan paused and continued. "I like to come
here to think and..."

"To experience the beauty?" Annie said. "To feel the
air and hear the crickets and see the stars?"

"Like it's all supposed to be this way. Strip away everything else, and this is what you have." Ryan stopped under a cottonwood, heavy with leaves. He took her hand.

Annie glanced away and grinned. He lifted her chin with a finger and stared into her black satin eyes. As he kissed her, he felt enchantment and excitement; she, a strange and wonderful electricity.

"I love you," he whispered as a frog croaked from bank.

She giggled but said nothing. Then, she kissed him, melding into him, her thighs joining his.

The embrace ended with a mutual sigh and gentle hug. "Let's walk a little further," Annie suggested. She paused and then with a moist hand, she took Ryan's and they walked on.

A park bench appeared in the dark ahead. Through the trees, the moon reflected off the thick murky veins of the slow moving water. Ryan led Annie to the wooden bench and, with a slight bow, invited her to sit.

"You're marvelous," he murmured, slipping his arm around her.

"It's beautiful here," she whispered. "And with you."

Her smile glowed in the dark; her floral body against his felt soft and sensual and blooming from the earth.

At the same time, she saw his eyes glowing, felt his smooth muscles and the sandpaper stubble of his face.

The two embraced, and a prairie storm of electricity spread through them.

They kissed and hugged, innocently and passionately, touching with tight caution.

"Let's go," Annie said, but as they walked to the car, they stopped under every tree and kissed and cuddled and pawed, entwined like liquid, like the old river and its ancient secrets.

***

The drive to Annie's house murmured and rushed, murmured and rushed. He, touching her knee as he drove; she, kissing him at every stoplight and touching his face at every sign. A fading floral smell lingered in the night.

As he turned into the gravel driveway at the house, he noticed the one-bulb porch light on. He remembered the sister and the church next door, but as he parked the car, the only thing he really thought about was the woman next to him. He looked at her, opened the window, and turned off the engine.

The moist air of the night, fresh with the timbered summer sighs of the nearby woods, crept into the car. Ryan leaned towards Annie, and they kissed, a touch at first, then mad, without inhibition as lovers.

Annie leaned back and looked into his mysterious blue eyes.

In the faint, rosy glow of the porch light, Ryan saw her enveloping smile and the rumpled blouse and her light brown skin now not timidly revealed.

As he kissed her, Annie closed her eyes and felt the button of her blouse open. His lips danced down her neck. She leaned back and, as she did, his mouth touched her damp and soft flesh straining for release from beneath her blouse.

"Don't, Ryan!" she cried. "Don't!"

He lifted his head slowly.

"Don't stop!" she sighed as she pressed his face into her fertile bosom.

Mark S. Darrah is a published essayist and short story writer. His fiction has appeared in *Cottonwood*, a literary journal published by the University of Kansas, and his performance mysteries have been successfully produced in various venues throughout the region. He has recently begun teaching writing as continuing education for Tulsa Community College. An attorney, Mark lives with his alluring wife, Jackie, and their wonder dog, Sammi.

The three hadn't always been enemies; adversaries perhaps—at least to begin with—but not enemies.

Circles of Guilt
by Trudy Graham

Huddled into a corner of the couch, Emma Crawley shook with anger, hurt, and frustration. Her silent shout seemed to ricochet around the room. A room which bore no visual clue to the turmoil raging within it, a room as emotionless as a stage set waiting for the curtain to rise, a room typical of the solid citizens in their sixties who lived in the West Tulsa home.

Emma's short white hair was still waved softly, but her floral print dress, usually crisp, was now wrinkled and unnaturally stretched.

Her husband quietly—too quietly—closed the front door. Short and spare, Harry Crawley's hair had receded far back on an already high forehead. Brown eyes blinked behind gold-framed spectacles. He held his body too controlled and still to be natural in his neat but casual shirt and trousers.

Guilty secrets! How did these dreadful things begin?

Harry's restrained voice reflected the tension of Emma's silent scream. "He killed her. Lane Summers killed our daughter just as surely as I stand here. I don't know how he did it, but he's a liar, a cheat, and now a murderer."

Emma recalled each word of the terrible scene just ended between her husband and their son-in-law. Lane had come to their house in response to Harry's urgent phone call.

Harry had been the spokesman, Emma by his side. He struggled to keep his voice quiet and steady. "Lane, a lawyer called us today. He says Paula was about to file for divorce."

"Divorce! That's ridiculous!"

"The lawyer said it was because of you and your women."

"What women? I don't have any women! I loved Paula. Would I lie about something like that? I haven't wanted to go on living since she died."

"Yes, you've lied," Harry answered, "first to Paula, and then to us. That lawyer had no reason for telling anything but the

135

truth. You sound guilty as all hell! I don't know how you did it, but somehow you caused my little girl to die!"

"You're calling me a murderer! I didn't kill her. I couldn't have. The doctors and the hospital would know it if I'd killed her."

"You found some way, you and your Indian tricks. But the disease center will find you out, and then everybody will know."

They stood there—enemies, the young man and his avenging in-laws—shaking with the frustration of unfinished battle. And then Lane stormed out of the house while Emma collapsed onto the couch.

The three hadn't always been enemies, adversaries perhaps—at least to begin with—but not enemies. Eventually they become close, almost parents and son, in spite of the early distrust.

Harry and Emma hadn't encouraged the relationship between Paula and this young man who was from a different background. They saw him as unreliable, even potentially dangerous to their only child.

Being older when she was born, perhaps Emma and Harry were over-protective of Paula. She thought so anyway. They tried to give her room. Sometimes they overdid that, too. Giving a 16-year-old a car wasn't unusual, but on a middle-class budget, a bright red sports car with a tendency to acquire speeding tickets was excessive.

Lane Summers admitted the car first drew his attention to Paula. It was a far cry from his beat-up truck, yet the truck suited his image better.

Lane wasn't a very big man—only 5'8" or so, about 150 pounds, with black hair and eyes and smooth dark skin. The wiry type, with calm eyes, but the kind of manner that let you know he was always on his guard; he didn't brawl, but you figured if he ever did fight, he'd know and use every dirty trick there was.

His lack of schooling embarrassed him. None of this "just be your own rough self" for him. No trying to better himself either. He just backed away with a chip on his shoulder. He would have liked to be better, a better talker, a better husband, have a better job with a better income, but he didn't want it enough to do something about it.

So opposite personalities carried an attraction that led to marriage in spite of her parents' misgivings. The marriage was probably described as average by most observers. Since they had no children, the couple was free to cruise the country music hangouts of Tulsa County in Lane's chosen uniform of blue jeans, plaid shirts, boots, and wide hats. Occasionally, he took Paula fishing, but his hunting trips were reserved for old cronies who shared his love for back-to-nature roughing it. Lane taught Paula to drink beer and smoke a little marijuana, but she knew little about most of his lifestyle.

"Before we got married, I worked on road crews, harvest gangs, and did some mechanical stuff," Lane told Paula. What he didn't tell her was that his interest didn't hold much past his next paycheck; that a lost job gave him the opportunity to do what he really wanted to do—hunt, fish, drink beer, and run around with his buddies, acquiring gas, food, and drinking money from welfare, Indian programs, or the working girls he picked up with ease.

But marriage changed Lane's life. Paula didn't have a lot of education, but she was a hard worker and had plenty of ambition. She landed a good job with a company in mid-town Tulsa, and after the marriage, she saw to it that Lane got and kept a job. Her parents provided a stability he'd never had. Lane's father had seldom worked, and his mother died in a mental hospital a couple of years after he married Paula. It seemed that sharing Harry and Emma became the couple's greatest strength.

After his mother's death, Lane sank into deep depression. Only the unlimited love and caring Harry and Emma poured out eased him through that black time. Lane demanded that same kind of care when Paula became ill and died—a corpse almost before she became a patient.

Paula's illness began while Lane was away on a sales trip. Hit by severe flu-like symptoms and a high temperature, her parents took her straight to St. Francis Hospital's emergency room where doctors hovered over her in intensive care. Tests revealed no answers, and medications provided little relief. One week to the day after she first became ill, Paula Summers died, and no one knew why.

Each survivor fought a separate hell. Again Lane dropped into depression and the Crawleys sublimated their own suffering to meet his continuing crises. He stopped working, seldom ate, wandered through the woods, and turned Paula's house into a shrine. Her clothes still hung in her closets, and her car sat in its usual spot, polished and filled with gas as though she would step out to drive it again at any moment. Worst were the middle-of-the night calls when a drunken Lane threatened suicide. Harry and Emma never failed to respond, burdened by the devotion he apparently felt for their daughter.

Burdened until a lawyer they had never heard of called to tell of Paula's plans for a divorce. Burdened until they knew Lane had lied about his devotion to Paula, that he had betrayed her over and over again.

Disbelief, then hurt, and finally anger overwhelmed them. Anger with themselves—at their gullibility. Anger with Lane. Anger even with Paula.

Harry exorcised his demons with loud talk and endless repetition of grievances. Emma held her sorrows inside. And like all animals of bitterness, the more they were fed, the stronger they became, held in check only until Harry and Emma could get some report from the Centers for Disease Control in Atlanta where the minutiae of a life and death had been sent, all except for the results of an autopsy, which Lane refused to allow because "he didn't want anyone to hurt Paula."

Just three days after their terrible confrontation a letter from Atlanta arrived.

"What does it say? It's from the Disease Center, isn't it?" Now that the answer was in their hands, Harry was afraid to open the envelope.

Emma's hands shook with all the unsteadiness of her sixty-five years as she unfolded the letter and read aloud the cold facts of their daughter's illness and death.

"So that's the way it was. We'd better get this letter right over to Lane," Harry said.

Her voice was shrill. "No! We will not hurry to my daughter's house to let her killer off scot-free!"

"He didn't kill her, Emma. The Disease Center says it was toxic shock."

"No! Atlanta just says 'reasonably sure.' Lane married Paula and made her miserable. Then when she was going to kick him out, she died. If I can make him suffer even one more day, I'll do it and be glad." *Guilty of everything else, Lane is surely responsible for Paula's death, too. And he must pay for it as I am paying.*

Emma recalled Harry's arguments against the marriage of their precious Paula to this half-wild Indian kid. That day as she'd listened, Harry's voice had become her father's, and instead of Paula, the girl standing by her sweetheart, was Emma herself next to Sam Fields. Sam's big hand almost crushed hers as he clenched it in repressed anger at her father's tirade.

She had turned to her mother, silently pleading for a word of support that did not come. In time, Sam went away, and eventually Emma married Harry Crawley, but she never forgave her mother.

Thirty years later, Emma had stopped Harry's tirade against Lane and persuaded him to support the marriage. Harry had tried, half-heartedly, to argue with her, but Emma, usually so gentle and agreeable, refused to accept his negative opinions.

Now twenty hours had dragged by from the time the postman delivered the letter until their sedan halted in front of Lane Summers' house on a hillside above the turnpike. Emma clenched the letter in her hand. The couple stepped out into the early sunshine, as oblivious of the fine morning as blind men facing a Rembrandt. Lane's pickup stood in the drive but Paula's car was gone.

"Maybe he's decided to put it in the garage," Harry said as he got out.

At the garage's narrow window, he cupped his hands around his eyes and peered through the small glass. He called to Emma and hurriedly reached for the door handle.

"I hear Paula's car running, Emma! Come quick!"

Exhaust fumes filled the garage. Harry coughed as he opened the door and turned off the engine. "Lane's still breathing, Emma! Call 911!"

***

Hours compressed into a few minutes as, once again, Emma and Harry stood next to an emergency room bed. A series of tubes were attached to the lifeless form. A nurse stood at one side and a doctor bent over his patient. He straightened and turned to them. "He's going to make it but ... a very close call. His good fortune is that you two came by."

Emma looked down at her hand still clutching the letter from Atlanta. Tears coursed down her cheeks. "This was what I wanted, you know. Lane ruined my baby's life. I wanted him to pay. Then I saw him lying in that car with their marriage license in his hand, and you yelled at me to call 911. I wanted to let him die, but I couldn't just let it happen. If I had, I would have been as guilty as Lane—full circle."

Gently, Emma opened Lane's hand and tucked the crumpled letter inside. She closed his fingers around the paper and turned away. "It's all over, Harry. Let's go home."

Trudy Graham is a lifelong Oklahoman and a resident of Tulsa since 1979. In the business world, she was manager of major word processing centers for more than 15 years. Writing in a wide range of genres—fiction, non-fiction, drama, anthologies, humor, and poetry, Trudy has received numerous awards in OWFI and Tulsa Friends of the Library competitions.

Jimmy was supposed to go job hunting this week, but Josh knew that wasn't going to happen.

The Snow Goose
by Laureen Gibson Gilroy

Josh really hated Jimmy. Not all the time. But sometimes, like now, when Jimmy would get crazy and wind up at Hillcrest Medical Center. Then Josh would get the call, and guilt would leap into his brain.

He's your mother's baby! You promised her you would take care of him! He's your little brother, for God's sake! "Oh, Christ!" he muttered, now I'm hearing voices.

The elevator door opened. Josh stepped out and automatically turned left. No need to look for a sign to show him the way to the psychiatric ward. He walked down the hall to the nurses' station and explained he was there to visit his brother. There was a song-and-dance routine about privacy laws then the nurse turned a couple of pages in the chart and found what she wanted.

"Looks like the meds haven't kicked in yet. When they do, I'll tell him you came by to see him," she offered.

"Any idea when that will be?"

"The doctor will have to write an order so your brother can have visitors. That won't be until tomorrow at the earliest. Rounds start at seven, unless the doctor is running late."

Josh looked down the hallway. "Is he locked up this time?"

"Yes. It's for his own good. He's hallucinating. Hearing voices."

"That hasn't happened in a long time."

He looked down the hallway one more time, then shuffled toward the elevator.

It was July in Tulsa. Hot. Hazy. Humid. Josh pushed the car door ajar. He waited while the steam cooled into air a man could breathe without scalding himself.

It never got this hot when we were kids. He's never going to get better. I should go make sure the house is locked up. Maybe get him some clothes.

141

Josh drove north past the jail then turned onto Edison. If only Jimmy were a gangbanger instead of a nutcase, he thought as the car approached Owen Park. There it was; the infamous pond with its resident waterfowl, most likely the direct descendents of the geese and ducks that swam there two decades ago when Josh and Jimmy were kids. He turned onto Quanah then took a right to swing by the Washington Irving monument. The obelisk was still there; a solid, phallic tribute to a great traveler and writer.

Holy shit!

A soccer ball bounced in front of the car with a kid close behind. Josh slammed on the brakes, and hit the horn. The blaring honk mixed with a woman's scream. The kid stopped and stared at Josh. The boy started shaking and was about to cry when the woman grabbed him and hugged him to her heart.

Josh's hand shook as he pressed the button to lower the passenger side window.

"You O.K., buddy?" Josh asked gently. The boy stared. His mother was kissing him and saying something Josh couldn't hear.

"Be careful next time, all right?" The brown eyes just stared back.

"Tenga cuidado, amigo," Josh said haltingly. The boy smiled and said, "Si, señor."

"Thank you, sir," the mother whispered, pushing the words past the fear in her throat.

Josh lit a cigarette then pressed the accelerator and drove down the hill. *Well, I guess the old neighborhood has changed.* He wondered what his father would have to say about Mexicans living on the same block. Josh had dated a Mexican girl for awhile. He learned the language and had thought about marrying her, but Jimmy, "El Loco," spoiled everything.

"Insanity runs in families," Mariquita had said the day they broke up. Memories of her brown eyes at dawn soothed Josh's mind.

She was so beautiful. Mariquita.

Josh took a final drag on the cigarette and slowed the car to a stop as he exhaled. There was the house where Josh and Jimmy grew up. *Check that. One of us grew up.*

It used to be the best-looking place on the block when their parents were still alive. The lawn had always been groomed and each season brought forth vibrant flowers to brighten everyone's spirits. Now the house depressed him. It wasn't run down, but it was plain. No flowers bordered the sidewalk or flanked the front door. In the backyard, the grass was yellowed and splotchy and needed watering. Shards of glass flashed in the sun like cheap diamonds. Josh looked up, and saw a piece of plywood covering the window in the back upstairs bedroom.

"Dude!"

"Timothy! Hey, thanks for taking care of that."

"No problem. It's just a patch 'til you can get it replaced. How's Jimbo? Did you see him?"

"They wouldn't let me. They've gotta get the drugs working first."

"Why don't you come over for supper? Ya hungry?"

"I guess."

"Shirley's cooking up some chicken fried steak. She's got some fresh corn, too. I checked the fridge in there to see if anything would spoil while Jimbo was laid up. Bunch of science experiments are in there, if you catch my drift. Come over to our place in about an hour. Shirley'll fix you up good. Homemade biscuits."

Josh hadn't thought about food since Timothy called him the previous evening. Neighbors had heard his brother screaming and glass breaking. When the police arrived, they found Jimmy in the bedroom curled up in a fetal position. He'd thrown a boom box through the back window. All he would say was "Don't shoot. Please don't shoot me, too." The cops took him to Hillcrest for an assessment just like they did after Dad died. Jimmy had gone crazy then, too.

Timothy went back to his house next door, and Josh walked into the old family home. The furniture was familiar, but the house looked like a bachelor's place. Spartan. Lonely. Timothy was right, the refrigerator was full of rotten, smelly food.

He went for days without eating whenever he stopped taking his meds. Why didn't he starve to death?

Josh climbed the stairs then stepped into the old bedroom. The bunk beds were gone, replaced with their parents' double bed, and the pellet rifle stood in the corner. A Crossman Air Gun with a Daisy scope. It felt like a toy now. Josh recalled how heavy it was when his father gave it to him on his tenth birthday. Jimmy was eight. One night, the boys decided to play coon hunters. They jumped from the window—the same one Jimmy broke out last night—and wormed their way to Owen Park. "Them dogs smell a coon for sure, brother," Josh said quietly. "Bet it's in that thar tree, brother," Jimmy replied. Josh spotted a squirrel, took careful aim and squeezed the trigger.

"Dang."

"My turn," Jimmy cried, grabbing for the rifle.

"No it ain't," Josh said, still in character. "I'm a gonna get us a turkey." He turned and began stalking the geese over by the pond.

"What are you doin' Josh?"

"Quiet!"

The older brother slid in another pellet, brought the rifle up, and pointed at the white goose. The rifle clunked as usual when fired, and the goose dropped immediately.

Both boys stared at the motionless bird.

"What did you do? Josh! What did you do?"

"I guess I killed it." Josh was stunned. He had never before hit anything he'd aimed at. The boys inched their way toward the bird. The goose lay on the ground as if sleeping. Josh squatted down and held up its head.

"It went through his eye. But there's no blood."

"Is he dead?"

Josh felt the goose's chest for a heartbeat. "Yup."

Jimmy sucked back tears.

"What are you crying for? It's just a bird. Help me hide the evidence."

The boys dragged the goose to the edge of the pond and rolled it into the water. It floated awhile and then sank.

"Jimmy, if you tell Mom and Dad, I'll kill you. You hear me? Stop crying."

He was so cute back then. The way his lower lip jutted out when he was angry or sad. His long eyelashes wet with tears. Why couldn't he stay like that? My sweet, adorable little brother. Why did he have to go crazy?

"Dude! Supper's ready!"

"OK. I'll be right over."

Josh put the rifle down and closed the bedroom door.

Jimmy was released from the hospital on Saturday, and he spent the night alone in the house. Sunday night, Josh drove over to see how he was doing. Jimmy was supposed to go job hunting this week, but Josh knew that wasn't going to happen. Every time Jimmy faced having to grow up and get a job, he would stop taking his meds or get drunk and go crazy. Josh was tired of taking care of his brother.

"Why did I promise you I'd take care of him? He's never going to get better. It's been almost a year, Mom, and I still can't believe you're gone. The doctors said it didn't look good—that you probably wouldn't make it. Time to get with my brother to settle things. I didn't believe them. You're dead. Jeez, why am I talking to you?" he shouted as he drove to the house.

After tonight, things would be different. He was going to put his foot down. Josh dropped his cigarette, stomped it out, and walked up to the house. It was dark. Pitch black. He knocked three times, then opened the door and walked inside. It was hotter in here than it was outside. Jimmy sat in the living room. In the dark.

"The electricity went off," he said, sounding the words slowly like a zombie.

"It's hotter than hell in here, Jimmy! Come on. Let's go to Braum's."

Jimmy leapt from the couch and ran to the car. They drove a few blocks to Braum's drive-thru and ordered two chocolate milkshakes. Of course, Josh paid. Before they got away from the cashier's window, Jimmy was begging Josh to take him to the park. Without saying a word, Josh swung the car out of the driveway and headed for the expressway. Jimmy laughed as Josh pushed the pedal to the metal all the way to the Quanah exit. Then Josh made the car crawl the rest of the way to the park while Jimmy begged him to hurry. They were both laughing now. Jimmy's eyes danced, and he pounded the dashboard.

Why can't he always be like this?

It was almost curfew, but Josh drove into the park anyway and stopped the car. They remained silent as they got out and strolled to the bridge. On each side stood rock walls, and Josh jumped on top of one while Jimmy climbed the other. Reacting to a starter's pistol that only they could hear, they ran along each wall, up and down, up and down, as the walls dipped and rose until they reached the tall points at the ends. Then they jumped off, crossed the street, Josh a bit ahead of Jimmy, jumped up on the other walls and ran up and down again, until ... suddenly Josh slipped and fell onto the grass. Jimmy kept running until he had won the race.

"Ha! I beat you! Josh. I won! I won! Josh? Are you O.K.?"

Jimmy leaned over his fallen brother.

"Boo!"

Jimmy gasped, then laughed right in Josh's face. "I beat you. Finally."

"I hope you're happy."

"Oh, yeah. This is the best day of my life! I beat you!"

Josh stood and brushed the debris off his cargo shorts.

"Remember that goose you killed?" Jimmy asked. "He keeps following me. He won't leave me alone. He keeps biting me and honking at me. He won't shut up. Why doesn't he come after you? You're the one who killed him!"

"Jesus Christ, Jimmy. No wonder they throw you in the loony bin. Talking like that. You sure sound crazy. A goose ghost chasing you! You're almost thirty years old. It's time for you to grow up. I can't take care of you forever, you know."

"You promised Mom you would."

Here comes the guilt. It's not going to work this time.

"Jimmy, I might not be around forever to take care of you. Did you ever think of that?"

That got his attention.

"You're not the only one who's been in the hospital, Jimmy. I've been gettin' some tests done. Doc says we should know next week. You better grow up, baby brother."

Josh turned away so Jimmy couldn't read his face, and pulled out a cigarette. He took a long hard pull, then exhaled two rings.

"Lung cancer?"

"What?"

"Do they think you got lung cancer?" Jimmy asked in a small, childlike voice.

"I don't know. Probably. They checked my lungs, my heart, my brain and, I swear, they took about two quarts of blood. My insurance better cover it."

Josh turned around to look at his younger brother. The gloating was over. Jimmy's eyes were big and trusting, just like when he was little. So trusting.

Josh walked over to the fishermen's pier.

"Let's see who can stay up on this rail the longest. We'll wrestle."

"Like the lumberjacks on TV?"

"That's right, little brother. Everything's legal."

Jimmy's face lit up as he climbed onto the railing. Josh got on the other end and they both inched their way toward the middle. Jimmy slapped at Josh, but missed and almost fell onto the pier floor. He got his balance and stepped back. They stood like prizefighters in a ring, looking for an opening, getting ready for the knockout punch. Suddenly, Josh lowered his head, stepped in then threw a roundhouse into Jimmy's head. His brother's jaw dropped, his arms fell limp as he tumbled over the side and into the water. Josh stared into the pond. The reflection from the streetlights made it difficult to see if any bubbles came up.

In five minutes it will be over. Five minutes. Wait. Wait.

Josh looked at the houses across the street then at the golf course. There was no one around. No one had seen him knock his brother into the pond. No witnesses.

It went just as he planned.

Calm down. Wait.

Laureen Gibson Gilroy is the Recycling Coordinator for the City of Tulsa, Oklahoma, and a member of the Dramatists Guild. From 1989-1995 she was a reporter for the *Tulsa World*. Her one-act play, *Don't Tell Anyone*, was produced by the Tulsa Junior College Community Theatre. Ms. Gilroy has also worked in the retail, entertainment, and health care industries.

What was going on? Where had all the people come from? What were they doing? Didn't they know that this was my lake? Mine and the swans?

Swan Song
by Valerie Gawthrop

From my window I looked down on the crowd gathered in one corner of Swan Lake. In contrast to the spectators, the lake itself was serene, the deep blue of the water broken only by the bright plumage of flocks of lazy, drifting waterfowl.

The birds were among the few delights left to me. I loved watching them ignore the noisy humans. If only I could get closer and feed the ducks with stale bread even though the signs forbade it... Somehow the signs restricting the waterfowls' diet reminded me of how fragile I'd become. What would happen if *I* were to eat the wrong crust of bread or swallow the wrong pill? Like the birds, I had become dependent on my keepers.

I pressed my nose against the cool glass. Soon I'd leave this window and walk along the path that I'd memorized over the weeks. I could already feel the hard concrete beneath my feet and smell the freshly mown grass bordering the sidewalk. *I can't wait to take off my slippers and run barefoot along the fence. Soon.*

My breath fogged the window. It was always so cold in here. Outside it was warm, hot even. The crowd below steamed in the sun.

I scanned the curving shore until my line of vision settled past the horde of people leaning over the fencing. There they were. I smiled as I recognized the startling white plumage of the pair of trumpeter swans that gave the lake its name. Nike was sitting on the nest I'd watched them build while Zeus marched up and down the fence, stopping to raise his head and stretch his neck at the crowd. His black beak opened, and I could imagine the harsh scolding call, like a medieval warning from a frustrated herald.

Zeus flapped his magnificent wings, and the air rippled around him. Joggers beware. Doggies back off. Spectators recoiled *en masse* as if assaulted by a singular blow. What was

148

going on? Where had all the people come from? What were they doing? Didn't they know that this was *my* lake? Mine and the swans?

Nike ruffled her feathers then twisted her graceful neck down and buried her beak into the straw. I flattened my palms against the glass. Of course. Why hadn't I realized sooner? What a time to be trapped in this miserable room. I balled my hands into fists and pounded against the window.

A sigh of air brushed the back of my neck. Someone had opened the door. I heard the squeak of rubber crocs on the tile floor. A tuneless whistle... I didn't turn around. A shadow fell across the wall. Someone hovered next to the bed. Fumbling with something. I heard the snap of rubber gloves, the rustle of plastic wrapping being ripped open. Beep, beep, beep the machines nagged. Never mind.

I pressed my cheek flat against the window and shuddered. My shallow breath made another circle of fog against the pane. Furiously, I wiped the window clean as if my very existence depended on a clear view of the lake. The machines surrounding my bed began to scream. Sunlight funneled into the room, and for a moment I felt as if I could ride the light like an elevator.

I clawed at the window, and the glass dissolved beneath my touch. All sense of direction deserted me, and I shook my head at the bewildering change in perspective. Instead of looking down at the lake from the twelfth floor, I stood facing the water, right in front of the swans' nest.

The crowd pressed around me as if I weren't there. Zeus was the only one who noticed me. He cocked his head my direction and opened his beak, but instead of a shrill warning his crowing held a proud ring. He turned and scooped the edge of the nest with his beak. I saw the tiny gray cygnet that was struggling to join its mother. Zeus nudged his newly hatched baby back into the nest but not before sending another proud call in my direction.

Nike spread her wings over the nest, covering the clutch of cygnets, shielding the hatchlings. I counted five, but it was impossible to tell exactly how many there were.

I stood on my tiptoes, surprised to discover that I was barefoot. "Good job, you two," I whispered. "Beautiful family."

The parents stared at me with their glassy black eyes. They heard. They understood. They recognized me. They knew I'd been watching them all this time. Waiting for the eggs to hatch—anticipating this bit of new life on the lake.

Now I could rest. I lowered myself to the bench next to the fence. It was cast iron but felt soft, warm. Only then did I dare look up. There it was, my room on the top floor of St. John Medical Center. The floor that held little hope and no comfort except for the view of the lake. My window. Was that a silhouette? Was someone watching? I leaned back, closed my eyes and soaked in the heat.

IV bags swung back into place on the stainless steel pole.

"Don't worry little one. God sent me." The nurse glanced at the Sharps container on the wall, ready to drop a used syringe into the plastic box. She hesitated. "Guess I better keep this stuff with me," she jammed the syringe and vial into her pocket. "Can't be too careful. I know my work is God's work, but it ain't hospital policy."

She leaned over the bed and smoothed the sheets over the still figure. "I just can't stand the way those heathen doctors have been filling you with poison, but no more." With a gloved hand she plumped the pillow then checked the industrial sized wall clock. "A few minutes, and it'll all be over. Swing low sweet chariot." A tuneless whistle…

"I'll stay with you as long as I can, but you gotta understand that I have to be out of here 'fore anyone knows that you've passed." She left the bed and began tidying up. Amazing how much junk accumulates in a hospital room, she thought.

"Tsk, tsk. How did these slippers get all the way over here by the window? It's been, what, a week, since you've been out of this bed?" She stared through the glass at the roof tiles crowning the neighboring building without seeing the slice of aqua blue that was barely visible through the gap between the brick walls and the traffic along Utica Avenue.

"You was fascinated by *something* down there but Lord knows I can't figure out what." She picked up the fuzzy blue house shoes. Alarms blared as the equipment registered death.

"Praise be, child. God almighty has claimed another of his flock. My work here is done for now," she said as the door whooshed closed behind her.

Valerie Gawthrop's work appears in several popular anthologies including *Chicken Soup for the Cat Lover's Soul*, *Sword and Sorceress*, and *Voices of the Heartland*. She's published nonfiction in a variety of national magazines and is the recipient of numerous writing awards. She is a member of the Oklahoma Writers' Federation Inc. and past president of the Tulsa NightWriters. Valerie has passed many pleasant moments watching the wildlife on Swan Lake.

She slapped five Ben Franklins on my desk. "A detective named
Kennedy told me you're Tulsa's best private investigator.

A Private Investigator Who Can Find Anything
by Art Youmans

When the stun gun's fifty-thousand volts hit me, I collapsed
like a rag doll on the backyard patio. I neither heard the robber
walk through the back door into my house nor felt him lift my
wallet.

The roar of the lawnmower had masked my cries for help. I
never saw the man who entered my backyard at dusk, who
yelled, "Freeze," and fired a Taser from a few feet away.

After I recovered, I staggered into the house and dialed 9-1-
1.

"My name is Tony Russo," I mumbled. "I've been mugged."

Then I noticed a poodle wearing a pink bow, its black eyes
staring at me from the hallway. "Get out of here!" I lunged, and
watched while the dog streaked out the open front door and
disappeared behind Siegi's Sausage Factory.

I slammed the door and went into the living room. The
contents of my desk were spilled on the floor, and I did a quick
inventory of what was missing.

A young patrolman arrived first at the scene. I explained
what happened and outlined the items that were stolen. I showed
him how the shooter entered through the back of my house and
exited by the front door. He took notes and turned to me.

"Are you sure the perp used a stun gun?"

"Hey! Take a look at my back. The S.O.B. sneaked up on
me." I took off my shirt to show him burn marks next to the
surgical scars. "It's sore as hell! I never got a good look at him."

"How did he get in your house?"

"It was my fault," I admitted. "Left the gate open and didn't
lock my back door when I came outside to mow. That was
dumb! Never do that again."

"Do you have registration numbers of the stolen guns, Mr.
Russo?"

"What's your name, son?"

"Dolan, Officer John Dolan."

"Well, Officer John Dolan, before retiring, I was Tulsa police detective Tony Russo. Of course, I have registration numbers. I'm an ex-cop, not a fool!"

"I've only been on the force for nine months. You must have retired before then."

"Yeah. When I hurt my back, the department retired me on a disability pension. I've been a private investigator ever since. Here's my P.I. license." I pulled out the card.

Dolan smiled and repeated the question.

"I had three guns inside ... two .38-caliber Smith & Wesson revolvers and a .32-caliber Beretta semiautomatic. I'd just finished cleaning them. The guns were in plain sight on my desk, next to the coin collection. Registration numbers for the guns and dates on the coins are on a sheet of paper in my safe deposit box. I'll bring the paper to headquarters tomorrow."

From the shadows a third man emerged. "Hey, Russo!"

Detective Joe Kennedy was short and stocky with his badge on his belt. He sported an Alfred E. Neumann grin. "I heard you say you got bushwhacked, big guy," Kennedy laughed.

Before Officer Dolan drove off in his patrol car, he had a chat with Detective Kennedy. When Kennedy learned I'd left the backyard open and the back door unlocked, he roared with laughter once more.

I glared at my former co-worker. All six-foot-five-inches of me hated Kennedy's sarcasm and lack of empathy. In his world, dumb crooks always robbed dumber victims. Life was a joke to this detective with his Don Rickles personality.

I slammed Kennedy into the side of the house. "One more wise remark," I growled, "and we'll need a homicide detective here. Do you want that?" I lowered the smaller man to the ground. "*Capisce?*"

"Hey," Kennedy said. "I'm sorry. Didn't mean to offend anyone...much less an ex-cop." He brushed off his suit. "Let's check inside and see what's missing from your house. Okay?"

I nodded

***

When the forensic technician finished dusting for fingerprints, Detective Kennedy made a few last note. "Tony," he asked, "is this accurate? The perp stole your wallet with twenty dollars and credit cards, three guns, a laptop computer, and ten Morgan silver dollars?"

"Yeah," I groaned.

"What's the total value?"

"About two grand. The silver dollars were in mint condition."

"Could you come down to headquarters tomorrow to check the crime report?"

"Sure. How about eleven in the morning?"

"Okay. See ya."

That night, I remembered an incident involving another private investigator in the college town of Oberlin, Ohio. A student stole the P.I.'s sign, which hung over the sidewalk in front of the investigator's office. In place of the sign, 'Confidential Detective Agency, I Can Find Anything,' the thief left a note taped to the office door: 'If you can find anything, find your sign.'

A local newspaper publicized the theft, and the student newspaper ridiculed it. Both publications printed the résumé of the P.I. and featured the name of the correspondence school from which he had received his investigator's diploma. For two weeks, the theft was front-page news.

The P.I.'s sign hung forty-feet above the floor in the student activity building. It would probably be there still except someone sent an anonymous note to the college president naming Tony Russo, quarterback of the football team, as ringleader of the prank.

The college president had to interrogate me, but I took the football coach along to vouch for my good character. Two days before the last game of the season, it was easy for the school's star athlete to deny any role in the mischief, even though I had orchestrated the prank with the rest of the team. When I went to the police station with the coach's wife, a lawyer, I denied everything. The investigation was old news a month later, and shortly thereafter, the P.I. shuttered his office and disappeared.

The same fate isn't going to befall me. It was a sick joke, but what the hell...I was a twenty-year-old kid then and didn't know beans about life. "I'll show the world what a real P.I. is like," I slapped my hand on the arm of my chair. "I'll find this perp, myself."

The next day, on the way to police headquarters, I stopped at the nearby McDonalds. My cousin was the manager.

"My silver dollar collection was stolen last night," I told him. "Would the order clerks and cashiers keep a lookout for anyone paying with new silver dollars?"

"We'll do it right away," he answered. "I'll focus the video cameras on the counter and drive-in window for the next few days."

Budget cuts in Tulsa had decimated the detective ranks. The police and fire department were managed with skeleton crews. *If I don't find the perp, no one will.*

"We'll do all we can," Detective Joe Kennedy said when he signed my statement.

"I won't hold my breath," I muttered. "Any problem if I investigate on my own?"

"Be my guest...but keep us in the loop. If you find the perp, let us arrest him."

"Yeah, sure."

I called every pawnshop within fifty miles of Tulsa, but the police had already faxed serial numbers with descriptions of the stolen weapons, laptop, and silver dollars.

At five that evening, I returned to my office and reviewed old case files. I pulled out a yellowed file sheet, and smiled. *Harry the Horse was my best snitch in the '90s; maybe he can help me now.*

I punched in his cell phone number.

"Harry speakin'."

"This is a voice from the past," I said. " I'm..."

"Detective Russo? Is that you?"

"It's ex-detective now. I had to retire. And, Harry, I need a favor."

"Hey! I owe you one. Don't know how you fixed it with the judge, but I got probation the last time they caught me takin' bets."

"It evened out. You helped the police, so we helped you."

"I appreciate it. Heard about your accident. That's tough."

"You get used to it, Harry." I told him about my last twenty-four hours.

"I've got contacts on the street," Harry muttered. "If the shooter's still around, we'll find him."

"Thanks."

"Remember it the next time I'm in the slammer."

"A youngster just came in to buy fries and two big Macs," my cousin whispered over the phone the next day. "He paid for his order with new silver dollars. Want to come down and see if they're yours?"

"Did you get the kid on tape?"

"Yep. He's twelve, and I know who he is—Detective Joe Kennedy's youngest son, Joshua."

"Cheezis! I'll be right there."

After I identified the coins, I gave my cousin six bucks in exchange for the silver dollars. After thanking him, I took the videotape and went home to think about my next step.

At my second beer, the phone rang.

"There's a punk at the bus station trying to sell some guns," Harry said. "A couple of .38 Smith & Wessons and a .32 Beretta."

"Is he a twelve-year old kid?"

"Naw! He's about twenty. You can't miss him. He's carrying a backpack... wearing blue gang colors, rings in his ears and nose. The kid's head is shaved like Mr. Clean. Better hurry! He's hyper. The punk may not stick around long."

"I'm on my way. Thanks."

***

Joe Kennedy Jr. tried to run when he saw me, but tripped on the curb. I was on top of him before he could escape. The hand-to-hand training I learned in the Police Academy came in handy. After a short attitude-adjustment session in the alley behind the bus station, young Joe apologized for shooting me with his Dad's Taser. I didn't hurt the kid but gave him the chewing out he deserved, and he paled visibly when I described what could happen to young people in jail.

I still held him in an arm lock when Joe nodded toward the backpack. "Your guns are in there," he admitted. "My brother, Josh, hid your other things in our attic."

"Call Josh!" I demanded, pulling out my cell phone. "Tell him to bring my stuff! We'll wait here for him."

"Okay," he hesitated. "Please don't tell my father, Sir!"

The laptop was working, and my credit cards were in the otherwise empty wallet. I checked the silver dollars and found five more missing. "These Morgan dollars are worth thirty-six bucks each," I said. "You owe me two-hundred-and-six dollars, fellows, including the twenty missing from my wallet and what you bought at McDonalds. How're you gonna pay me back?"

"We're broke," the oldest brother whined. "I spent your dough on a video game."

"Tell you what. Do you guys know how to mow a lawn?"

"Sure."

"Okay. Here's my plan." After I explained, they stared at each other for a moment, then nodded.

That afternoon, I called the police chief and told him everything had been returned, anonymously. The case was closed.

A month later, Detective Joe Kennedy phoned me. "Tony, I appreciate you giving Joe Jr. and Joshua a job cutting your lawn this summer. Both boys have grown up a lot since they've been working for you. Joe Jr. used to be a lazy kid looking for an easy buck. Now he's thinking of studying criminal justice in college and becoming a cop, like his old man. Joshua also wants to be in law enforcement. Whatever you said to my kids shaped them up. My oldest even ditched the body piercing. Thanks, Tony!"

"When I was twenty and a college student, Joe," I admitted, "I did a few things wrong. That's when I decided to become a cop. I wanted to keep people from making the same mistakes I did. Good luck to the boys."

That night before going to sleep, I looked into a full-length mirror in the bedroom. "When I knock on the Pearly Gates," I said, chuckling. "And tell them about helping Joe Jr., Joshua, and Harry the Horse... St. Peter will have to let me in."

When I awoke in the morning, I felt like a twenty-year-old, again.

After breakfast, I walked to my office. The sign, 'Tony Russo, Private Investigator, I Can Find Anything,' hung over the front door.

I was smiling when a platinum blonde walked in at ten. "Can you really find anything?" she asked sweetly.

I nodded. The blonde was the type of woman I'd fantasized about in my dreams—a beauty queen who bulged in all the right places.

She slapped five Ben Franklins on my desk. "A detective named Kennedy told me you're Tulsa's best private investigator. Please, Mr. Russo, find my dog! His name is Max." She handed me a color photo of the forty-pound male poodle, adorned with a large pink bow on its head.

No wonder the mutt ran away. If anyone put a pink bow on my head, I'd have taken off, too.

"Ma'am, call me Tony. You've already paid my five-hundred-dollar retainer. I also charge $250 a day plus expenses. Is a dog named Max worth that much to you?" *The mutt's probably still hanging around the dumpster behind Siegi's Sausage Factory.*

"That poodle's a millionaire," she explained. "I nearly passed out when the lawyer explained the disposition of assets in my boyfriend's trust. He left half his estate to me when he died. The mansion and other half went to Max. If that dog disappears for more than a month, or dies from anything but natural causes, Max's income to run the estate goes to charity, and the mansion will be sold. I won't have a roof over my head. I'll do *anything* to get him back."

I stared at her green eyes, sparkling like emeralds. *After I find the poodle and collect my expenses, I'm asking this babe for a date. Maybe she really meant it when she said she'd do anything for the guy who got Max back.*

"If the poodle is still in Tulsa, I'll track him down." I tried to look as confident as Humphrey Bogart did as private eye Sam Spade in *The Maltese Falcon*. "Tony Russo can find anything... even a millionaire dog named Max."

Art Youmans is a published writer of both fiction and non-fiction stories and articles. He's won numerous writing awards in the mystery/crime genre, as well the 2006 Oklahoma Writers Federation Nostalgia Contest, and Sleuth Ink's May 2006 Mystery/Crime Writing Competition.

The uniformed cop said it was my fault, but what does a green kid like that know anyway?

Judgement Call in Tulsa
by Jackie King

The boy's death wasn't my fault. It took a ton of money and even more string-pulling, but the judge finally exonerated me completely. I never spent too much time worrying about the outcome—feeling confident from the beginning that everything would work out—I'm used to getting my own way. What surprised the hell out of me was that I also convinced my secretary. It was her teenaged son that I killed.

It happened last year, and I have to admit that for awhile Mary went around the office looking pretty pissed. Then all of a sudden her anger disappeared, and she was back to her usual self again. Well, maybe her face seemed a little different, but at least she didn't look mad anymore. Just sort of blank, like most of the suckers in this world.

Nothing affected Mary's work. I knew it wouldn't. She's the best secretary I ever had or could hope to have. My business was small when I first rented an office on the north side of Tulsa, but with Mary's help, I soon developed a huge clientele. She runs my whole office all by herself, and I mean everything. Answers the phone, keeps my books any way I tell her to, and takes dictation. I sent her to school, and she knows all about computers, too. I hate the things. I prefer to just lean back in my chair, put my feet up, and tell Mary what I want done.

Now I know that I'm a lucky guy to have such a secretary, but the truth is I deserve it. Fifteen years ago Mary's husband deserted her and left her with no marketable skills and a year-old kid to raise. I was the only one willing to give her a job. Mary came in temporarily to help out with the filing. I had two women back then, and both of them together couldn't put out the work Mary does now.

I could see right away that she was smart as a whip, so I sent her to Tulsa Community College at night to learn typing and all of that stuff. So you can see that Mary owes me a lot. And you'd better believe that I remind her of that debt, too.

160

Bobby was the kid's name. He ran with a bad crowd and was always in trouble with the cops for smoking pot or shoplifting. It was his own fault that he got killed. His car ran out of gas, and he was refilling his tank right there on Highway I-244. I don't care if he had pulled over on the shoulder; the darn kid should have had sense enough to turn on his hazard lights. And don't give me that crap about it being in the middle of the day. If he'd had those blinkers on, I would never have hit him, and that's the truth.

The uniformed cop said it was my fault, but what does a green kid like that know anyway? I had a talk with my buddy, who's a high-up official, and the rookie soon shut his trap.

Anyway, my lawyers got it all straightened out in court, and alcohol was never even mentioned. I explained to the judge that I have diabetes and passed out driving my car. I made a big deal of how bad I felt. But if a guy's sick it's not his fault. Is it? Of course, I didn't mention taking prescription medication and then drinking all those beers. A guy's got to know when to quit talking. It's all a matter of good judgment.

The whole mess was a damned nuisance, anyway. Court took way more time than I had to spare.

After the death of her son I was good to Mary, even though she gave me dirty looks during the trial. Right after the verdict I gave her a week off without pay so she could get her act together. That shows what a good guy I am. I told her so, too.

I figured she'd quit working for me, but she didn't. I have to say I sure was relieved. If she knew what a good secretary she really was, I'd have to pay her a whole lot more money. I've always figured if she threatened to leave I'd double or even triple her salary just to keep her. She's that good. But I'm too shrewd a businessman to give anything but a three-percent-a-year raise without a good reason.

I started out collecting bad debts when I was just out of college and built what I figured was a temporary job into a million dollar business. I'm smart that way. The only mistake I ever made was taking on Amos Smith as a partner. Of course, there wasn't much I could do about that. He was in the car with me on the day of the accident, and he swore in court that I'd only had one beer. The price for his perjury was making him my partner.

As soon as Smith was on board, things went downhill. Every decision he made cost me a small fortune. My blood runs cold just thinking about it. I wanted to talk it over with Mary, her being so smart about solving problems, but I figured she wouldn't want to listen.

Well, as it turns out, I was wrong. One morning she brought the subject up herself. She'd just brought me my coffee, and we were standing in my glassed-in office.

"Mr. Elrod," she said, "Mr. Smith is going to run this company right into the ground." She always spoke in cliches like some dumb hick who didn't know anything. Cracked me up since I knew she had a mind like a steel trap. This came in real useful in my business. Mary would just fade into the woodwork during a business meeting, and then afterward she would have a smart solution for whatever problem had been discussed.

"Mr. Smith's smart mouth ticked off the chief administrator of the Southside Medical Center this afternoon," she said. "It looks like we might lose their account."

I gritted my teeth and listened to Mary tell the details of yet another Smith fiasco.

"I've had just about enough of Mr. Smith's boo-boos," she said. "I don't want *my* job threatened by someone so stupid he's ruining all of the hard work that you and I have done together. This town is full of downsizing companies. After the recent crashes, it would be almost impossible for a woman my age to get a job around here."

It was all I could do to keep from grinning. I'd fed her that line for years. It's a good way to keep the help humble.

"We've got a problem, for sure," I said honestly. Then without so much as blinking I shifted gears and lied with a straight face. "If I can't lower the overhead, I won't be able to afford to give you one of those nice raises this year."

We both looked through the glass and into Smith's office. He was sitting with his feet on the desk reading the sports section, acting like he was me.

"I'm tired of not having any control over my life," Mary said. "I've thought about it a lot, and I'm going to fix the problem."

I figured that was just so much hot air and drove home to watch a few porno movies. I have quite a collection, and this is how I entertain myself these days. I'm in the middle of divorcing my middle-aged wife, so I'm real careful not to visit my girlfriend, Bambi. Plenty of time for that after I've gotten the divorce arrangement I want.

On the way into the office the next morning I turned on the seven o'clock news and learned someone had slipped into Smith's house the night before and shot him dead. His wife found his body when she got home from her book club meeting. There were no suspects.

For a minute I couldn't breathe. Did Mary kill the guy to save my business? Then I laughed. Naw, I thought. Not Mary. What a crazy idea. Smith was bound to have all sorts of enemies.

I'd just settled behind my desk when Mary walked into my office with a cup of coffee in one hand and a paper sack in the other.

"Well," she said, just as cool as could be. "I did it. I solved our problem. I killed Mr. Smith last night." She set the coffee down then slid a .38 out of the sack right onto my desk. I almost fainted.

"Mary!" I shouted. "Have you lost your mind?"

She shrugged.

"I just don't much care anymore," she said. "I was determined not to be out of a job. Even if they arrest me, I'll have a place to stay. It doesn't matter to me. You can call the police right now if you want."

"Now hold on there a minute, Mary," I wiped the sweat off my forehead and pondered where I could stash that gun permanently. "You know I'd never be able to manage the books without you. I don't have a clue how anything really runs in this office. Anyway, you've been under a lot of pressure lately. I don't think this is entirely your fault. I think it was just temporary insanity, and everyone knows you shouldn't go to jail for that."

"Maybe you're right." Mary brushed a wisp of graying hair away from her face. "What do you think I should do?" she asked.

"Where did you get that gun?" I asked. "Can it be traced to you?"

"Not in a million years," Mary said. "I have my contacts. Bobby's friends, you know."

"Did you leave fingerprints?" I asked.

"Of course not," she said, calm as if we were discussing ordering office supplies. "I watch enough *Law and Order* to know about those things. I only look stupid."

That was a true statement if I'd ever heard one, and I smiled.

"Then give me the damned gun," I said. "I'll get rid of it for you. The police will come around and ask questions, but don't say any more than you have to. Play dumb. You know, act like it's a meeting with a client. Leave everything to me; it's easy to get out of things when you know how."

It was a minute before Mary spoke.

"I'll never mention it again." She used a pencil to push the gun toward me, and I slipped it into my briefcase. Tonight I'd wipe off my own prints, right before I dropped it into Keystone Lake west of town. No way was I going to lose the best office help I'd ever had. Anyway, Smith deserved to die, the bastard.

I gulped down my coffee, then decided I had to get out of the office and away from Mary. I don't mind admitting that she had me pretty spooked. I told her I was calling on Southside Medical Center and that I'd be back in a couple of hours. Then I picked up my briefcase and left.

The traffic was heavy. There was a pile-up on the Broken Arrow Expressway and it took me over an hour to drive across town. Then smoothing things over with the client took another couple of hours. Back at the office, I got out of the car, and two men wearing cheap suits walked up beside me.

"My name is Sergeant Perkins, and we need you to take a little ride down to the police station with us," the guy wearing navy polyester said.

"What?" I asked. "What are you talking about? I'm not going anywhere with you." I started to walk away, but Perkins grabbed my arm and held on like a snapping turtle.

"We're investigating the murder of Amos Smith," Perkins said. "Can you tell me what you were doing last night?"

"I was home watching a video," I said, planning on how to ruin this jerk's pitiful career. "And get out of my way or I'll have your job."

"Was anyone with you last night?" Perkins asked.

"No, I was alone." I gave the guy a sneer meant to shrivel him down to size, but the arrogant bastard didn't even bat an eyelash. Well, I'd show him. "You should know that I play poker with the police chief every Tuesday night," I said looking him straight in the eye so he'd get my meaning.

"Is that so?" Perkins asked and took my briefcase from me.

"Hey! You can't do that! That's private property. You can't look in there without a search warrant." My pulse didn't even skip a beat. I knew more about the law than most lawyers.

"You mean like this one?" Perkins slipped a paper out of his inside breast pocket and handed it to me before snapping open my briefcase. He pulled out the paper sack and peered inside.

"Yup," he said to his partner. "Looks like this is a .38, all right." He sniffed the gun. "And recently fired, too. Just like that anonymous tip said."

Jackie King is a full-time, published writer who lives in Tulsa, Oklahoma and entertains herself by murdering, on paper, the people she dislikes. She is a member of numerous writing organizations including Sisters in Crime, Mystery Writers of America, and Romance Writers of America. She has two novellas in print. Her first mystery, "The Spinster, the Pig, and the Orphan," is in the anthology *Foxy Statehood Hens and Murder Most Fowl*. Another novella, "Flirting at Fifty," appeared in the anthology, *Chik~Lit for Foxy Hens*. She has published dozens of short stories and articles about women and women's problems.

Really, the whole situation just fell into place as if it were meant to be. And maybe it was.

An Oklahoma Kind of Evening
by Peggy Moss Fielding

She wasn't really worried. She was from Tulsa and her guilt came from an Oklahoma conscience working overtime. No one cared what they did. Not in New York City. Hidden affairs were surely common as dirt up here in the Big Apple. Not to mention that she felt common as dirt to be doing such a thing. She just couldn't help herself.

It had all been so easy. There was a place for them to meet Fridays, never anyone else around. They could leave separately and no one the wiser. Really, the whole situation just fell into place as if it were meant to be. And maybe it was. When she'd learned that Clyde was working in New York, it had been almost impossible to keep herself from calling him. Finally he'd called...and the rest, as they say, was history.

Their first meeting in New York City was burned into her memory, as was their previous relationship as childhood pals and classmates when they usually shared a desk in class or a table in the cafeteria at lunchtime.

They were true-blue Okies, surrounded by thousands of New Yorkers. She and Clyde comforted each other, in ways that only another Oklahoman would understand. The Conference Suite in her building was perfect for their secret activities. Neither was willing to drop their weekly meeting, never mind Clyde's wife's objections. Her own husband was not a problem. In fact, her New York City-born husband encouraged her. He gave her permission to meet with Clyde so long as she slept in the guest room when she returned home and did not require a kiss the next morning.

"There are just some things I can't be expected to do for you," he'd explained.

Each week she could hardly wait. She turned on all the lights, put country-western CD's on the player, and checked their private meeting area. A real Tulsa, Oklahoma evening for a man and a woman getting back to their origins. Sharing a common taste. Together.

They followed the same pattern each week. He loosened his tie and took off his suit coat. She slipped out of her heels and took off her jacket as well. The delicious scents in the conference rooms commanded their avid attention.

Pinto beans with ham hocks, fried potatoes, cornbread, and Dr. Pepper. While they ate, they talked about home, read letters and part of the Tulsa World. Just a little Oklahoma evening—downhome food, music and news. That evening kept them sane for the stressful week to come when they had to function as fast-moving, good-smelling New York business people, twenty-four hours a day.

Nobody cared...nobody but the two of them.

They'd started with sharing the red or white or golden globes, highpoint of their evening, but they had graduated to each having a globe of their own. Naturally. They were still Okies. Deprived Okies, except for this one night. On this night they went home satiated. On this night they each devoured, along with the beans, the potatoes, and the cornbread, a whole raw onion of their own!

Longtime Tulsa NightWriter, Peggy Moss Fielding lives amongst a pack of feral cats in midtown Tulsa, Oklahoma. She writes full time and has sold a number of articles, short stories, nonfiction books, and novels. Nowadays she writes novellas as a part of the *Foxy Hen* flock, where she is sometimes referred to as "The Mother Hen."

Mike flailed the water to a froth. Time was running out.

Sounds of Silence
by Charles W. Sasser

Twice a loon cried out from some lonely and hidden cove, the voice of the earth's soul—or so it seemed to Mike. He lifted his head and the loon fell silent. Only water gnawing at the boat disturbed the quiet of the Canadian north woods. Men, as they grew old, came to know and expect the sounds of silence.

Mike lowered his head. Squinting, he knotted a weedless silver spoon onto his fishing line. Thick fingers gnarled from a lifetime of labor made it difficult to work with thready six-pound line. The line was light for Northern Pike, but all God's critters deserved a sporting chance. Mike often chided Harv about his "carp pole" and his rope-like line.

"Work the weed beds," Harv had advised.

Mike had been up in the chill pre-dawn to kindle a wood fire in the stove; Harv's circulation was bad, and he got chilled easily. He stepped out onto the tiny screened porch to watch color from the un-risen sun spill slowly across the still lake between timbered shores. Patches of shredded fog hovered low. Mosquitoes hummed.

He went back inside. The wood stove rumbled heat. He put coffee on to boil, and scrambled eggs and fried bacon crisp the way Harv's wife did before she passed away. He stirred flour and milk into hot bacon grease and made gravy to go with biscuits fresh from the oven. The aromas of a camp breakfast filled the primitive cabin.

"You always cooked as good as any woman, Mike," Harv said from the bunkroom. "That's the only reason I've come up here with you every spring for the past thirty years. I'd marry you—except you is so ugly."

Harv had no appetite. Mike ate breakfast alone, saving some for Harv later on. Harv had coffee in his bunk.

"Fog'll burn off soon," Harv said. "Fish the sheltered coves where there's structure. That's where the big pike are."

"First, I'll catch another walleye for dinner."

"Walleye are sissy fish. They bite like crappie."

"They're sweeter-tasting."

"Don't waste your time, Mike."

Mike had brought in a walleye for dinner the past two days. Harv had had no appetite.

"Moby Pike," Harv said. "Concentrate on him."

Harv had always talked of their catching a *really big* pike—a Moby Pike.

"There ain't much time left, Mike."

"Don't talk that way, Harv."

Mike caught another nice walleye anyhow, hoping that after it was golden brown in tonight's skillet the food would entice Harv. He hooked it in the deep cut between the two lakes. It was a fat fish, firm and dark and still lively in the fish basket. Then he started working the weed beds in the inlets where big Northern hung out this time of year.

He tucked the silver spoon into flat dark pockets of water trimmed in lily pads and sprigged with needle grass that stuck up from the surface like spikes. He worked around felled logs, sticking up boulders, and beaver dens. Once he spotted a muskrat swimming, and then a bald eagle eyed him from the top of a fir. Morning mist burned away, and he looked across the lake, narrow at this point, and saw the log cabin all blond in the sun and perched above the little dock where the spare boat was tied. A gull swaggered across the decking, waiting for fish scraps.

Harv sat on the screened porch where Mike left him propped in a chair with pillows. Mike flailed the water to a froth. Time was running out.

"Mike, catch him," Harv had said.

"Maybe you'll catch him yourself next year."

"No," Harv said.

"The bigger fish are females. Did you know that, Harv?" Mike asked. "They can live up to twenty-five years. Females live longer than males."

"I don't give a rat's ass, Mike. I want to see you catch it."

Before he left to fish, Mike carried Harv to the outhouse around back. Harv had once lifted the rear end of a jeep so Mike could change a flat tire. Now, he weighed about ninety pounds and was as frail and brittle as a sick wren. Mike tugged Harv's underwear down to his ankles and lowered him onto the hole.

The procedure embarrassed both of them, but Mike tried not to let on. Harv stared at his bare feet.

"I'll wait outside," Mike said. "If you—"

"Mike, I can wipe my own ass, for God's sake."

Mike fished some more. He felt the eyes of his old friend watching him from the cabin.

"Did you hear the loon this morning?" Harv had asked, looking across the lake from the screened porch.

"Maybe we'll hear it later."

Mike listened for the loon to cry again as he fished. The loon was quiet. Harv's seat at the other end of the boat was empty. That was what life was all about, it seemed—empty seats. Females did not always live longer than males, even though that might be some rule. Harv's wife Mary went first. Then Connie was next.

The silence of the loon and the silence of empty seats mocked him.

Mike fished within sight of the cabin where Harv could see him. He worked the bank back and forth, casting into the inlet where Harv had caught the thirty six-incher four or five springs ago. Water nibbled at the boat. Braided line hissed off the reel when he cast. The silver spoon plopped when it landed in the water. The soft grind of the reel on retrieve seemed to whisper secrets from the past.

Mike and Harv went to school together in Tulsa, Oklahoma. They dated and married best friends, Mary and Connie. They were each other's best man. They worked midnight shifts and lived on the same block. They were godfather's for each other's kids. They attended their wives' funerals together.

The Otter pilot at Nakina had not wanted to fly them in to the lake this year, not with Harv having to be carried down to the seaplane wrapped in a blanket—haunting, feverish eyes and bones with yellow parchment stretched over them. Mike slipped the pilot an extra C-note.

"You'll be isolated for a week," the pilot cautioned. "There's no phone or other means of summoning help. Wait until the ol' chap feels better, eh?"

"We can't wait," Mike said.

The pilot looked at Harv trembling and wrapped in his blanket. "Why are you doing this?" he asked Mike.

"He's my buddy."

"Yes," the pilot said.

He looked at the C-note. He looked at Harv. He looked back at Mike.

"Load him aboard. He must be one hell of a friend, eh?"

Mike cast and retrieved, cast and retrieved, covering the weed beds in the cove and always within sight of the cabin. He avoided looking at the empty boat seat. He still couldn't look at Connie's chair back home. He glanced sometimes toward the cabin. Once, he held up his hand and studied the ancient, twisted thing like he'd never seen it before. He drank water from a bottle, listened for the loon, and went back to fishing.

He had caught plenty of twenty-to-thirty-inch Northerns the past two days, but the old Grandmaw of forty inches or above that would qualify as Harv's Moby Pike eluded him. Harv was disappointed.

"Use my rod and reel," he had suggested last night. "It's my lucky Shakespeare."

"With forty-pound carp line to make it lucky."

"Darrell says carp need loving too."

"We could use it to anchor the boat."

"Don't give the bitch a chance, Mike. Not this time."

Mike switched to the Shakespeare. He fished and ate a sandwich for lunch. Peanut butter and mayonnaise on rye. He'd left a sandwich and ice water in a thermos next to Harv on the porch. He doubted Harv would do much more than nibble at it.

The sun burned straight overhead and brassy on the water, like reflecting into a mirror. Mike drank some more water and fished with greater resolve, even a certain desperation.

Most truly big fish hit when least expected, as though to catch the angler after boredom and routine have set in. Mike sat hunched over and staring at the water, slowly cranking his reel, thinking of nothing in particular and wanting to go on thinking of nothing in particular, simply going through the motions. The point of his rod twitched once. The spoon hung up on a weed? Then the pike hit so hard it almost jerked the rod out of his relaxed hand.

He yelped in surprise and caught the rod before it got away. At the same time he sprang to his feet, precariously balancing himself as the boat rocked from side to side. Harv's heavy rod bent almost to the snapping point, vibrating. Line burned off the drag as the fish made its strong run across the front edge of the weed beds. Mike played it, not daring to horse it, not even with Harv's carp line.

The fish erupted from the dark depths in a furious display, gills rattling, head shaking in a desperate attempt to throw the lure. A sleek, long body of a fish, dark on top, the color of the lake, sparkles of silver on the sides, with a full pearl underbelly. Mouth of teeth like an Arkansas River gar or a Suwannee 'gator.

Mike's hands shook and his heart pounded as he coaxed it to his landing net. It was almost too big to fit into the net. He got it in finally, head first with its fluted wild tail beating the rim. Mike threw down the rod and used both hands on the net handle to heave the monster over the gunwale and dump it into the bottom of the boat. It stretched all the way across and pounded either side of the boat with its head and tail.

Moby Pike! Good thing he caught it on Harv's Shakespeare. He pivoted toward the cabin and threw wide his arms in triumph and excitement. He was laughing and shouting at the same time.

"Harv! Are you looking, buddy? We done it, Harv. We done it!"

He cranked over the outboard and throttled it wide open. He could hardly wait for Harv to see Moby close up. He almost crashed into the dock before he got shut down. The wake caught up and thudded the boat against the dock, nearly tossing Mike out into the lake. He hung a line over a post and, grabbing the fish in both arms, leaped out of the boat and started running up to the cabin trail with the weight of the pike out in front so Harv could see it.

"Harv! We done it, ol' son!"

The fish's wide tail dragged in the dirt. Her black eyes glowered fiercely.

"Harv?"

No reply came from the cabin porch, although Harv was still sitting where Mike left him. Mike could see him through the sun-glazed screen.

His step faltered. He stopped. The fish struggled in his arms.
"Harv?"

He looked back toward the lake, wishing he could turn time
back to some previous spring on the lake when ol' Harv would
come striding up behind him wearing that silly grin and flashing
his mischievous eyes. Boat wake still bashed against the shore
and the dock, banging and slamming the boats.

The lake turned smooth and brassy again while Mike stood
there frozen in time. Silence returned. Finally, with a sigh, he
walked slowly to the cabin, carrying the fish as it gasped for life.
He opened the screen door. Harv sat propped in the chair with
his eyes wide open, but the chair was empty.

"Did you see her, Harv?"

That was all he could think to say.

After awhile, he carried the fish back down to the dock and
worked it back and forth in the water until it revived. He released
it and remained kneeling on the dock until the fish regained its
equilibrium and swam away. From some lonely and hidden cove
the loon listened to the earth's soul and cried out twice more.

**Charles W. Sasser has been a full-time freelance
writer/journalist/photographer since 1979. He has published
more than 50 books and over 3,000 magazine articles and
short stories. His books have been translated into Spanish,
French, Chinese, Russian, and Serbian, among others. His
bio is included in *Who's Who in the World.***

Order additional copies of *Shades of Tulsa* online at AWOCBooks.com.

Call or write for pricing on multiple copies to:

Dan Case
AWOC.COM
P.O. Box 2819
Denton TX 76202

940-395-2836

Printed in the United States
200118BV00003B/172-621/A